CW00530680

Face to
No-Face

Face to No-Face
Rediscovering Our Original Nature

Dialogues with Douglas E. Harding

Edited by David Lang

InnerDirections
P U B L I S H I N G

The publisher gratefully acknowledges the kind help
of the Napa Yoga Center and the California Institute
of Contemporary Arts in contributing toward
the publication of this book

InnerDirections Publishing

INNER DIRECTIONS FOUNDATION

P.O. Box 130070, Carlsbad, California 92013

Phone: (800) 545-9118

www.InnerDirections.org

Copyright © 2000 by David Lang

All rights reserved. No portion of this book may be
reproduced in any form or by any means without written
permission of the publisher.

First Edition

Printed in Canada on recycled paper

Book & cover design by Joan Greenblatt

ISBN: 1-878019-15-5

Library of Congress Catalog Card Number: 00-105745

For Richard

Contents

Preface

Douglas E. Harding has written many fine books to share his message about Who we really are. His most popular, *On Having No Head*, has been in print continuously since 1961 and is widely regarded as a classic in the field. In each of his books, Harding writes with flair and precision about the ease and simplicity of experiencing our true nature and the implications of living life in the light of that experience. Indeed, he is so effective as a writer that it is quite common for readers to "get the point"—or see Who they really are—from the books alone.

And yet Harding is not only a writer. He is also an accomplished speaker. Even in his nineties, he spends much of the year leading workshops around the world with his wife, Catherine, from Britain to the U.S., from Australia to Japan, from Canada to France. His message in his workshops, of course, is the same as his message in his books: that it is the easiest thing in the world to see Who you really are. But the presentation style is different: less formal, more spontaneous, drawing on personal experience more frequently than his writing does.

Thus the purpose of this book: to bring to readers the other side of Harding—Harding the public speaker, Harding the workshop leader, Harding the conversationalist. Drawn from many hours of audiotaped workshops, small group meetings, and interviews which took place between 1983 and 1999, these "talks" attempt to capture on paper Harding's voice. I hope that, as you read, you will be able to feel Harding's presence, enjoy his stories, appreciate his wit, and benefit from his wisdom.

I would like to thank Golden Gate University in San Francisco for its support of the project; my brother, Richard Lang, for a transcript of an interview he conducted with Harding and for his constant encouragement; Dan Clurman for his invaluable feedback and for a tape of Harding speaking; David Robin also for a tape; Rebecca Turk for the gift of her transcribing machine; Virginia Parsell and Robert Wolf for their careful editorial and proofreading suggestions—Virginia also for her enthusiasm about an early draft; Carol Fusco for her loving support throughout the project and beyond; and Douglas Harding, not only for his editorial suggestions and illustrations but also for his friendship and his wisdom.

—David Lang

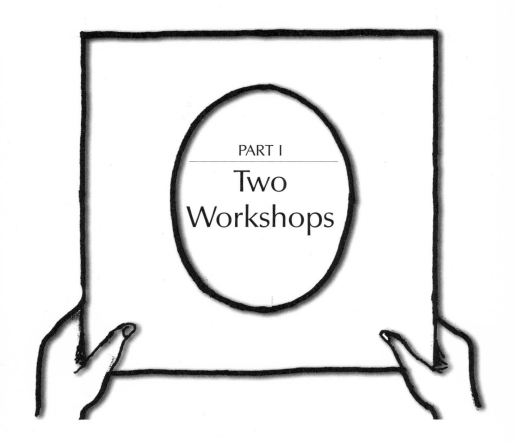

PART I

Two
Workshops

Chapter One
Workshop I

Today I want to strike an autobiographical note by way of introduction. My reason for doing this is that all genuine communication about spiritual matters is based on experience and not on just book stuff. Also, I had some very grievous problems when I was in my teens and my twenties, and it may be that some of you have similar problems. You don't look to me as though you have many problems, but I hope you've got some problems because they're the most helpful thing of all, aren't they? They are motives for looking for the place where problems cannot penetrate.

Take Douglas at the tender age of twenty-one. I had been

brought up in an ultra-fundamentalist, evangelical sect in Suffolk, England, called the Exclusive Plymouth Brethren, a sect where to read Dickens I had to lock myself in the WC, otherwise the book was burnt. We had schoolbooks, but any other books my father ceremonially burnt because they probably proceeded from the Devil. At twenty-one, much to my father's agony and distress, I broke away from the Plymouth Brethren.

My first problem was connected with the fact that I had inherited from my father—rather than from this sect—something of immense value, which I will treasure to the end of my days. It was the intuition, the feeling, the certainty that the power behind the world is self-giving love. My darling father lived and died in this belief. He was very narrow and bigoted, but he was a dear man who had this deep conviction. I knew my father was right, but I couldn't accept the theology or the way of life of the sect. At twenty-one I'd never been to the theatre, I'd never been to the cinema, and I wasn't allowed to read anything except the Bible. My problem was, how could I live in the light of this wonderful view that, in spite of the enormous appearance to the contrary, love is at the heart of the world, without believing, as Alice said, six impossible things before breakfast? That was problem number one—a very grievous problem, but a problem which had possibilities lurking.

The second problem was one which probably very few of you here have, looking at you. It was that I was so self-conscious. I was paralytic with self-consciousness. I'd go into a room with strangers, and I would be sweating and trembling with fear at the impossibility of facing this crowd of people. I was incredibly shy—not nice, shrinking-violet shy but aggressive shy, which is the most horrible of all because you're angry with people if they don't look at you and you're terribly upset if they do look at you. It's a double bind. I thought I was the ugliest person in

4

Chapter One

Christendom. I wasn't, but I thought I was. My nose in particular was so absolutely disgusting; it stuck out. I took it into a room, everyone looked at it, and it worried me terribly. I hope none of you have the experience as severely as I had it. It was ridiculous, but it was the case. You notice I've recovered from this second problem.

The third problem was the aimlessness of my life. I had nothing to structure my time, nothing to live for, nothing to die for. I was at a loose end, trying one thing after another.

Well, those were my three main problems: my inability to find out how it was and why it was that love was behind the world (if it was indeed true, which I knew it was in my guts), my appearance and shyness, and the lack of meaning in my life.

But I did have one thing going for me in spite of the problems: a feeling of surprise. I've always been gifted with astonishment and gratitude at having happened into the world, and the determination not to live and die without having a look at what has happened. You see, having occurred, it's a pity, a terrible shame, to take everybody's word for what has occurred, to take everybody's word for what it's like Here, and never to bother to look for myself until I'm no longer around to have a look. I was absolutely astonished and thankful at having occurred. I needn't have occurred, but I had occurred, and I had to have a look in spite of these nasty, nasty problems, which persisted in some degree up to when I was around thirty years old.

So, I did have that going for me. I was in India at the time, working on Who I really, really, really am. I had been working on this problem for some months because at the heart of the heart of the matter, my feeling was that we are built for love, we are love, we are identical with what Dante calls "the love that moves the sun and the other stars"—the final words of the *Paradiso*. I felt there was a mystery behind my existence connected with this view of my dear father that Who we really, really, really are is linked with, is even identical with, the power behind the world, which is alleged to be self-giving love. I knew that this was true, but how could it be?

What I am perceived to be, I said to myself at that time, depends on where you're looking at me from. I decided that what I am is a function—excuse the rather formal way of expressing this—a function of the range of the observer. In other words, if you look at me from ten feet away, you say, "Hi, Douglas" because you're at the right distance. You're where Douglas is on show, where you hold your camera to take a picture of Douglas. If you come nearer to me, of course, you lose Douglas. I am like a mandala or nest of concentric circles, and if you bring your camera up to one of the nearer circles or regions surrounding my center, you come to a place where you get a photograph of a patch of skin, or an eye, or lips, which are not exactly Douglas, are they? If you come nearer, searching for Who I really, really am, this indwelling Mystery, you come to regions where you can get actual photographs of cells, giant protein molecules, smaller molecules, and so on. Then, physicists assure me, the story is one of atoms and particles. And you are still not Here. Atoms are almost empty space. God knows what particles are or where they are. They're practically nothing, aren't they? Now what is at the center Here? That's what I was looking for. I was looking for what was beneath the electron. I had a question: What is at the center? I couldn't make it beyond the electron. That was as far as I could get. Quarks weren't invented sixty years ago.

Then going further away from Douglas instead of approaching him, but still looking at the place where I am, your story is of this city here. Going still further, you get a picture of California, then America, then the Earth, and then still retreating but still looking Here, you get a photograph of the Solar System, the

Chapter One

Galaxy, the Galaxy shrinking to a point, and in the end, practically open space.

So whether you come as near as you can to Here or go as far away as possible, the story is of Space, with the human region in the middle. What I am depends on where you are regarding me from. In fact, I consider myself from all these ranges. I feel myself into these various regions. Sometimes I feel like just Douglas—miserable, old, selfish, small, self-regarding Douglas. Other times I feel like my family. People die for their city. People died for the city of Athens, didn't they? People die for their country. They're more their country than they are that little guy. And then there are times when I want to shed the whole darn lot, and I just shut my eyes and say, "Keep out, world. Enough is enough." I retreat into Who I am right Here. I am nothing whatever to do with that external stuff. In fact, intrinsically, I am Nothing, aware of itself as Nothing.

Well, one identifies with any of these regions. One's particular appearance depends on how far the observer is away. I'd got as far as understanding that, but my trouble still remained, my self-consciousness, those selfish, ridiculous, absurd anxieties.

Then I noticed something which I'm going to share with you in the experiments in a moment. I was looking Here, trying to find out what was Here, at the root, central to this place. I happened to be in the Himalayas. There [pointing up] were the wonderful Himalayas. I looked down from the sky and the mountains, and in the nearer valleys I could see some grass. Closer still I saw Douglas's feet and Douglas's tummy. But I found I just stopped here at my chest. Above my chest was Everest. I stopped here as Douglas, and I was replaced by the scene. I simply noticed that I had no head. Crazy, isn't it? Well, it's not quite accurate because I should say I didn't have a head *Here*. Of course I had a head, but I kept it about a meter away in the bathroom mirror. Here, I didn't have a head, and instead of my head I had Kitchunjunga and Everest.

And then I thought, what a crazy thing! Gosh, Douglas, what did you think before you saw this? Did you think you were stuck in the dark, wet, sticky mess of an eight-inch meatball? Did you think that? Come on, Douglas, you didn't think that ever, did you? You were always busted wide open for the world. And of course it was obvious. When I was very little I was like this. I was busted wide open for the world. Then when I grew up, I did a naughty, stupid, and ill-mannered thing. In order to join the human club, I took that little Douglas in the mirror and enlarged him, turned him round, and put him on my shoulders, which of course I can't do, and I walked about in the world as though there were a meatball Here to keep the world out with. If I had a friend in front of me, I said silently, "Keep out! I've got one!" But I haven't got one. I find absolutely nothing Here whatever.

Now, we'll just interlard this brief autobiography with an experiment so that we share this experience. Be sure not to look at me when you do it.

Will you look at your finger, which is the great instrument we employ here, and look at what your finger is pointing at? Start off by pointing at the ceiling. You will see that your finger is a thing, and it is pointing at another thing. It may be a light-fitting. They've both got color, they've both got shape, and they've both got position. Your finger is pointing at a thing.

Now bring your finger down, and point to the wall just below the ceiling. Again, what you are pointing at has color, just like your finger has color, and it has shape, just like your finger has shape. So it's thing to thing, isn't it?

Chapter One

Now bring your finger further down, and just because I'm handy, you can point at Douglas's head now. You are pointing at a rather decayed and ancient meatball with a beard on it. Now point to Douglas's body. There he is, the right way up, the head at the top and the tummy and so on below it.

Now turn your finger round and point down to the floor. You will see again a thing indicating a thing, a colored finger pointing at a colored floor. Now point to your lap, will you please, and you've got the same story. Now point to your tummy. For God's sake, don't look at me. Look at your finger. It's about a foot away from your tummy. You can see again it's thing to thing. The finger's a certain color, and the tummy's another. Now point to your chest. It's much the same, isn't it?

Now point to what's above your chest. *Point to what you're looking out of.* What is your finger pointing at now, on present evidence, when you drop imagination, drop conditioning, dare to be your own authority, and look at where you're coming from? What is your finger pointing at? Is it pointing at an object, a solid, small, limited thing for relating to those other things out there, or is it pointing at Room for those things out there? Is it pointing at Capacity? Keep your finger in position now, would you, and keep looking at your finger, but primarily look at what your finger's pointing at. Isn't what it's pointing at boundless, going on and on forever? Isn't what it's pointing at totally transparent and speckless? And isn't this speckless, boundless Capacity in receipt of the scene, of the room, of the wall, and what you were looking at? Because it is empty of the scene, isn't it absolutely united with the scene? Isn't it awake? Isn't it alive to itself? Will you find Awakeness anywhere in the world but Here? Isn't this where Awareness or Awakeness or *I Amness* belongs? Does it belong anywhere but Here? You're the authority.

We are always looking AT things. What the blazes are we looking OUT OF? The great German poet, Rainer Maria Rilke, said, "And we spectators always, always looking at things, never out of something. Who's turned us round like that?"

"Ah," you may say, "looking at things, that's really looking. Looking at No-thing, that's not really looking." I think that it's the other way round and that when I look at a thing, I only glimpse it. A thing is so darned complicated. First of all, I only see the front of it. I don't see the sides or the back. I don't see the inside. I have to scan it because it's so complex. I can't take it all in. In the same way, I only glimpse the world. The world is in this sense invisible to me. But when I look Here, I see This with absolute authority and clarity. This is the true vision. Hence Shen Hui, a Chinese master of the ninth or tenth century, said, "Seeing into our Void nature, seeing into No-thingness, this is the true seeing, this is the eternal seeing." To see Who your finger is pointing at, to see Who you are is more evident, more authentic, more complete, more truly seeing than seeing your finger, or anything else in the world. The only thing we can really know is Who we really are. Of course, Who you are remains totally mysterious. But there's nothing Here to go wrong about. It is Clarity itself. Who we really, really, really are is a Piece of Cake. It's presented. It's obvious. Isn't it absolutely obvious?

One last thing: you looked up (in fact, down) your body, and you found a place, a line, where things switched over into No-thing; where the world switched over from what it looked like to where it's coming from; where you ended as a person and began as your True Self or No-self or True Nature; where your form, which is for looking at, became the Void, which is for looking with. Now could you draw a line with your finger across your shirt or blouse where it fades away? It's as though the moths have been at your shirt and have chewed the top of it off. Draw a line there, and then raise and spread your arms until they are horizontal. Don't these arms extend the line you drew? They are God's arms. When they come from a human being, when they're sticking out of a head and shoulders, as they do for other people, the hands are human. But when they're sticking out from this Clarity, this Absence, then they really are the arms of God. You are putting your arms round the universe. Your hands are as far apart as East is from West, aren't they? An enormous distance apart. Your arms really go to the edge of the world. Aren't your arms the arms of Love itself?

When I was young, we had a little homily: "Man's extremity is God's opportunity." Isn't this your extremity? This is very concrete, isn't it, where your humanness switches over into your Godliness, your Buddhaness, your True Nature? Doesn't it occur in this magic place only? We never look at this place. Of course, it doesn't apply to other people, only to you who switch over, flip over from what you look like to what you are. There it is. What are you looking out of now?

You have now been with me in this experience and shared it perfectly because there's only one way to see this and to share it, and that is to perfection. You can't half see this Clarity or see a spotty Clarity. It is a perfect experience. It is an all-or-nothing experience, and you did it just as Douglas did it and the Buddha did it and Jesus did it. Just the same.

To continue with my little story: I tried to share this experience with people because it was so surprising. Some people thought I was very profound and rather interesting and talked symbolically and that I was a wonderful mystic who saw things that were hidden from people in general. But most people just thought I was plain bonkers. They thought I was crazy. On the other hand, I was getting rather less shy, for there was nothing

Here to be looked at. I could go into a room and, gosh, I was the room. I had all those faces. I didn't feel under inspection anymore. But for eighteen years—a long time, it's rather a sob story—for eighteen years I failed to show anybody This at all. I was very bad at conveying it, I suppose. I didn't have the experiments. I was not as faithful or as clear about how to share It as I am now, but I should have shared It. My fault, not other people's fault.

However, in the middle of those eighteen years, I made friends. The trouble with the friends was that they were dead, and they'd been dead a long time, and they'd been dead in China also. But they were good friends. They were the Zen (or, rather, Chan) masters of the Tang and Sung dynasties in ancient China, and they said that our blessing, our enlightenment, our freedom, our liberation, our treasure is in one thing. It is in looking to see what your face looks like.

I read the story of a boy called Hui Neng, who turned up in a monastery in the south of China. He was illiterate, poor, and young, but he happened to see what you've just seen. He wasn't very articulate about it. In the monastery were five hundred holy monks meditating away like nobody's business, and this poor boy wasn't even allowed in the monastery. He was only allowed in the kitchen, pounding rice. But he was clear about what we've just seen.

Now, the master of that monastery was about to die and needed a successor. So he started a competition, and he found out that the boy in the kitchen had the answer. The master sent for this boy at night and said, "Chum, you are the new abbot. Now you must run for it because all these holy monks will be after you." The master rowed the boy across the river, gave him the bowl and the robe which were the insignia of office, and Hui Neng was then the absentee but true abbot.

However, one nasty monk caught him up. The monk was

prepared if necessary to kill Hui Neng to get the insignia of office and make himself the abbot. But Hui Neng said, "You don't want that silly old bowl or that silly old robe. What you want is to find your treasure and your liberation, your enlightenment, the answer to your problems." The monk said, "Yes, Master, show me!" And Hui Neng showed this chap, who was a retired general, what you have just seen. The monk looked. He did what you did just now, exactly what you did. He sweated and trembled a bit, because presumably he'd been meditating twenty years to see this darn thing, and he was surprised. So he said, "Oooh!"

But then he had second thoughts, just as you've had second thoughts. (Haven't you said to yourself, "Well, this is very clear, but it can't be what the Buddha and enlightenment are about. It can't be as simple and easy as that.") So the monk said, "Tell me the rest, Master." But Hui Neng said, "No, you've got it. That's it. What you do with it is important, but that's it."

So I got some comfort. I didn't have any living friends, but I had some dead ones. Other characters in Zen were also helpful. There was another boy, who was also uneducated and poor, both great advantages. (All that book-knowledge and sophistication is a terrible disadvantage. I hope you haven't read very much.) In this second story, a young boy, Tung Shan, is reading the most holy scripture of Mahayana Buddhism, the *Heart Sutra*, with his master. It starts off by saying, "Here, form is void, but the void also is form. Here are no eyes, no nose, no mouth, no ears, no tongue, no functions of those organs," da da da da da—a little bit of packing. And then it says, "Therefore the Bodhisattva ceases to tremble, for what can go wrong?" It ends with, "Hooray!" in Sanskrit. That's "Wow!" in American.

The boy said to himself, "I don't understand. The Buddha says this. He wouldn't lie." Then he looked at his master and said, "Master, you've got eyes and nose and mouth. I've got eyes

and nose and mouth. The Buddha wouldn't lie. I don't understand." The master said, "I don't understand either. You'd better
go and see another master." So Tung Shan went off, and he looked
for masters. He went on year after year looking for someone to
explain the *Heart Sutra* to him, where the Buddha says you don't
have any eyes and nose and mouth. One
day he was walking over a little bridge. The
water was clear in the river, and he looked
down into the water. What did he see in
the water? He saw where he kept his eyes
and nose and mouth. He saw where he kept
his human face. Of course, *you* don't usually
look for your face in a river. You look for it in
the mirror on your bathroom wall, don't
you? But it's the same thing. Now when
you go home, would you do something
for me, please? Would you look at the
face in the mirror and just be honest
about where it is and which way round it's looking?

Tung Shan saw that his face was there in the water, and he
saw what the Buddha meant. He saw his *human* face there, and
he saw his *true* face Here. This is what Zen Buddhism calls the
Original Face. I have two faces. One is my human face, which is
my appearance. It's a meter away, and I give it to you because it
doesn't belong to me. It's your property. You're welcome to the
darn thing! When I take it from you, I'm committing larceny.
What we do is take our appearance, which belongs on other
people's shoulders, put it Here on our own shoulders, and then
wonder why we're so messed up. So there was Tung Shan, finding his human face a meter away from his real Face, the Face he
had before his parents were born.

The real Face, this Clarity, is the Face of the One we really,

really, really, really are. In my terms, it's the Face of God. It's the Face of Allah, the Face of the *Atman-Brahman*, the Face where the world is coming from. And it is absolutely speckless, clear, imperishable. It's impersonal. You can't take credit for it. It's got no labels, no laundry marks. Tung Shan saw this, and he became the founder of Soto Zen, which is the largest school of Zen at this time. So all of you are equipped to find and even to found some incredibly wonderful thing like Soto Zen! Congratulations!

To go back to my autobiography. I didn't care too much if I didn't share my Original Face with my contemporaries because I shared it with some noncontemporaries whom I respected enormously. It was very, very heartening. But since then I've managed to share it with a few people, including you, my good friends, here this afternoon.

As for the problems I talked about—Douglas's personal hang-ups as a young man—just a word about them. I found it was quite a time before I lost this head-thing for looking out of. Little Douglas at two had been No-thing-for-looking-out-of-and-for-enjoying-the-world. Then he grew up and became a thing-for-looking-at. Now, thanks to seeing my true Face Here, I become again No-thing-for-looking-out-of. And the problem of shyness, all that terrific ego-trip, which blinds you to people and gets in the way of love, was, in principle, solved. But it took a few years, I can tell you, before the Freedom here established itself and became not a thing-for-looking-at but No-thing-for-looking-out-of.

Now what about the Love that I was looking for at the heart of the world? Society, of course, runs on the model of confrontation, which is the opposite of love. Language says that you and I are face to face, that we confront each other. Personal relationships are said to be relations between A and B. They're symmetrical, aren't they? You have a person here and a person there and something going on between them. That is the model of our social setup. It says that you and I are face to face.

We are now going to investigate in the next experiment whether this model of confrontation is true or not. If it's not true, we'd better change our minds about personal relationships. It could be that our society is in deep trouble just because it's not telling the truth about what personal relationships are really like. Are they confrontations, or are they something quite different?

However, it's terribly, terribly hard to see what we see. We see what we are told to see, what's policy to see, what is allowed that we shall see, what language determines we shall see. We are conditioned to experience what society has set up. In the next experiment, the Paper Bag, we are going to ensure we are deconditioned sufficiently to have a fresh look and see what's really going on. We are going to look at a familiar thing in an unfamiliar context.

Our parents and teachers and language all say, when we meet someone in the supermarket, we are face to face with that person. As a result, we *see* ourselves as face to face with that person. Well, suppose we met someone not in the supermarket but in one of the bags of the supermarket. That would be very unusual, wouldn't it? Then we would be in terrible danger of seeing what's actually going on.

We have, therefore, imported at great cost and trouble from Australia some supermarket bags! What you are going to do is meet a friend in one of them. Why are we doing this crazy thing? We are doing this crazy thing to see whether it is true that we confront people symmetrically, face to face. We have been told what to see in the supermarket. We have *not* been told what to see in the bag of the supermarket. In this context, it's easy to see what we see. So freedom and love creep in.

However, let me first issue some warnings. When we go in

the paper bag with our friend, we are not going in there in order to have a mystical experience, to find the heavens alight with joy. That's not the purpose. Of course, if it happens, that's all right! It's lovely, but it's not the purpose. Nor are we going in the bag to fall in love with the person opposite, though that is not absolutely forbidden. Nor are we going in the bag to stare into that person's eyes. Any feature—a nose, a chin—will do. And we're not going into the bag to have a special feeling about that person. We're going into the bag, I hope, just to address one simple question: *Have we ever confronted anyone?* We are not going to investigate all that feeling stuff, which is ever-changing and all over the place, but the simple question of whether we are confronting one another in there, or anywhere.

I will ask a few questions while you are in the bag with your partner. These questions are not for answering out loud. They are to help you arrive at your own answer. When we go in the bag with our friend, it is to tell the truth about what is given now, not what we think, not what we feel, not what we remember, but what is actually on show. *On present evidence* is the key. Please put your face into the bag.

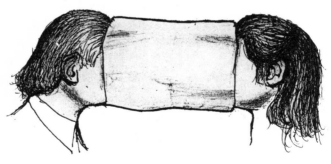

The first question is: How many faces are given, on present evidence, in the bag? The second question is: Are you face to face in there, or is it face-at-the-far-end to Space-at-the-near-end?

The third is: Have you ever been face to face with anyone in your whole life?

Now, keeping our faces in the same relative position, could we just lower the bag? We don't need the bag now to see that it's face to Space and that you are not, not, not confronting that person; that you are still, without benefit of the bag, empty, clear Space, Capacity for that friend; and that you haven't a darn thing to keep that one out with, not a speck to keep that one out with.

All right, let's go back in the bag for further investigation. Let's study in some detail what we have here in the bag. Look, for instance, at the color of those eyes, those lips, those cheeks, and that complexion. How could you possibly register and take in that color if you had any color whatever? Are you not colorless for that color?

Now look at all that complexity over there, at the eyebrows and the eyes and the lips and the rest of that rugged terrain there. Isn't it on show in the absolute Simplicity at the near end? Is there any complexity at the near end? In order to take in that scene at the far end in any detail, you have to start at the top and keep scanning across, back and forth, as you work down to the eyes and the nose and the mouth and the chin, and by the time you've got to the chin, the top of the face has all gone fuzzy. It takes time to take that one in. But you don't need any time to take in the near end, which is absolutely visible in an instant, in its clarity and its simplicity, all of it on show perfectly.

At the far end of the bag, the face you see has a certain age— young, old, or somewhere in between. At the near end of the bag is our Original Face. It is the Face of the One we really, really are. Are there any lines on it? Could this Face ever perish? Could it get older? What is the age of the One at your end? Surely the One at the near end has the Eternal Face of Who you really, really are, the Imperishable Face of the Reality behind the universe.

Another thing: you see how that face at the far end is limited. It's got a line round it. But your Space has no boundaries. It hasn't got a hard line round it like the face at the far end has.

And finally, before we come out for another breather, you see how solid and opaque the face is at the far end. But isn't the near end absolutely clear, more transparent than glass?

In other words, to sum up, isn't what you're getting at the far end the exact opposite in all respects of what you're getting at the near end?

Now we lower the bag again but keep our faces in the same position, and see that we don't need the bag in order to have this vision. Could this not be a totally different way of life: to be always open for that person, whether that person is your friend, your enemy, your husband, your wife, your child? You are busted, busted, busted wide open for that one, whether you like it or not, if you are telling the truth. Isn't this honesty the basis of love? Aren't you giving your life for your friend, not because you're a nice person but because you're a truthful person and you see that you have *died to* what is at the near end of the bag and have been *resurrected as* what is at the far end? This is a most beautiful thing. Surely the truth behind this sorry old confrontational world of ours is love, just as I felt it was and was told it was when I was very small. We are built to die for each other, to disappear in each other's favor. We are built for loving.

The world runs on confrontation like our cars run on gas, and it's a lie. Never for one second have you been face to face with anyone in your life. It's always been face to No-face. I repeat: Have you ever, ever, ever confronted anyone in your whole life? Hasn't it always been like this: face there, Space Here?

Now let's go in the bag for the last time. This bag is like a cream separator or centrifuge. You are the center of this machine. It's whirling round at great pace, and all the material, the cream or butter has gone to the far end, and the near end, the center Here, is clear of anything and everything. At the near end, you've got all the Awareness, and at the far end you've got all that which it is aware of. The near end is free of form, of all that solid stuff, and the far end is free of all that spooky stuff, free of consciousness.

You say, "Come on, Douglas! My friend at the far end is *not* devoid of consciousness, in my experience. Surely that's a very stupid and naughty assertion!" I say: OK, but *where* will you find the consciousness of the one at the far end? Will you find it by peeking into her or his eyes, into those black pupils? Will you find two little basilisks or hobgoblins or fairies of consciousness lurking behind those eyes? I think not. Where will you find the consciousness of that one, the one who says 'I am'? Where will you find that? Or is it totally inaccessible to you?

Well, if, whilst still looking at the one at the far end, you attend to the near end, you will notice that the Space at the near end is awake. It's absolutely alive to itself, fully conscious, and it's conscious of itself as No-thing, as colorless, featureless, totally empty and totally full. The Space is conscious of itself at the near end, *but it has no personal characteristics*. It doesn't have any of your laundry marks on it, and it is no more your property than it is the property of the one at the far end. It will do for both of you. So I'm suggesting, and it is only a suggestion, that you could really say to your friend now at the far end, "Thank you very much. You've given me your appearance, and that's a wonderful gift. There I *have* your appearance; here I *am* your Reality—because your Reality is that very same Consciousness which is my own Reality Here."

We can now lower the bag for the last time, and we can see that this is the situation. That friend of yours has given you her or his face, and Here you are the Reality of that friend, her or his inside story. That's double intimacy—not the feeling of love but the fact of intimacy, which makes love possible and which encourages love and gives love a chance.

We're built to this fabulous design. Everybody, however vehemently they deny the truth, is built to this fantastic pattern. The real world (could I call it God's world?) is based on the mystery and delight and beauty of self-giving love, just as I felt it was and knew it was and was told it was when I was very little.

Having found this way in to Who I really am—seeing that my human face belonged in the mirror and to other people, seeing that I was built for loving, not because I was a nice old Douglas but just because I was noticing the way I was built—having seen this, was it the end of the story? Rather it was the beginning of my true biography. The initial seeing of your Original Face is something you can't do wrong. It's perfect seeing. You've got it. But what you do with it is another matter. Well, what did I do with it? Where did I go from this vision? I began to practice it, slowly. That's why I was eighteen years waiting to share it with people.

What is the practicing of it? It's pure pleasure. It's not that hard, old, miserable, meditational grind which we give up because it's so dull. It's easy and natural. It is practical in all the circumstances of life, especially when you have someone in front of you. But whatever the occasion, don't lose touch with Who you are. Whatever you are perceiving or dealing with over there, don't lose touch with or sight of where you're coming from right Here. It's two-way looking: object there, subject—Who you really, really, really are—Here, as in the bag. In the bag you were looking at the far end and the near end simultaneously. Life is like a great big paper bag. This is meditation.

You say, "It isn't, Douglas! Meditation is folding your legs, etc." Well, I'm not against folding your legs, etc. It might be extremely helpful for you, sitting there and doing the traditional meditational practices, but it was not what I found helpful. What

I did instead seemed to be also rather like some other people's ways, people whom I respected very, very much. What is this way, which I suggest you might consider? This way is: whatever the circumstances, attend in both directions. This is a practice that can establish you in Who you really, really are. It takes some work, but it's the most pleasurable work I know. Here, meditation is enjoying the world and the Enjoyer of the world simultaneously. And it is enjoying the world and the Enjoyer of the world *now* rather than doing something with a view to enjoyment in seventeen lifetimes.

All sorts of surprises come to you when you attend This way as well as that. You have terrific fun, and you also find that you have a lot more energy. You take the cork out. Your end of the paper bag, Who you really, really are, is the fountainhead, surely, of all energy. When we block it up with a head, we are obstructing the flow of that energy and inspiration and a great deal of joy, too. We hallucinate a thing-Here-for-keeping-the-world-out-with at great cost in energy. It takes an enormous amount of energy to hallucinate and creep into a meatball. That's why we get so tired. If we want a little more energy, we will stop investing it in this hallucination. Of course, the energy's not only consumed by building this thing-Here-to-keep-the-world-out-with but also by adjusting this thing to every person we meet. I've got to put on a different face for you and for him and for her, worrying about what people are making of it. There's no energy left for enjoyment of the world and Yourself, Who you really, really are.

The effort put into seeing Who you really, really, really are will be differently rewarded in each case. I'm not making specific promises as to how it will work out in your case. The first thing is to see Who you are, which you've all just done. Congratulations! The second step is to go on practicing it till it's

Chapter One

natural to be natural.

Yes. What we're on about is simply being natural, being the way we are, stopping lying, stopping hallucinating, being ordinary—not funny, weird little mystical creatures floating about on cloud nine. This is having your feet on the earth, enjoying the world, enjoying people, enjoying life. It's being the way we are instead of being the way we were told we are. That's all. All of us are already living from this. The whole world is doing it right. What is wrong is that people don't notice they're doing it right! Everybody is living from Who they are. But we bung ourselves up with this imaginary block Here, and that's crazy.

So the second stage is to practice it. How do you know you don't have a special gift for enjoying this, and that after only a brief time it will become your style? Whatever is happening you are centered, and you're living from Who you really are. There are many ways of practicing this attention. The great reminder is when you've got someone in front of you. Shall you lie and say it's confrontation, or shall you tell the truth and see it's face to Space? Then love can flourish. I am not saying that this guarantees love but that telling the truth gives love a much better chance.

There are all sorts of other ways. Everything is pointing you back. One of the most fascinating, beautiful things about Who you really, really, really are is that you never moved. That's most peculiar. You never moved! Not an inch! Now the guy in the mirror rushes around like a frenzied ant. We talk about the speed of modern life and all the tensions building up, and we rush around the world because we think we are *in* the world. We have no peace, no interior tranquility. We are coming from agitation, *and it's a lie.* If you don't believe me, get in your car and just see whether Santa Cruz is dancing or not. You will find that the telegraph poles are all preaching to you the gospel of your stillness.

Aristotle said, "God is the unmoved mover of Santa Cruz—no, no, of the world." Get in your car and tell the truth: Are you moving, or is Santa Cruz dancing? Are the buildings still and you moving? Or is the truth the other way round, that you are still and that the telegraph poles are going by, the buildings are dancing, and the near hills are sliding against the far ones. The whole scene is being shuffled like a pack of cards. Santa Cruz is a much happier place when it dances—and when it leaves you at rest. I can't believe how we can edit out the fact that we are still and the world is moving. It's extraordinary, our capacity for hallucination and self-deception!

When we were very, very little and told the truth, and we went for a ride with Daddy in his car, we had such fun. It was carnival time. California danced. Even England danced! And then we grew up, and we got into double trouble. The world ground to a halt. But where did the commotion go? Where did all that movement go? It went into ourselves. We lost our peace of mind; we lost our tranquility. All that commotion crept in Here, and it was a lie. Now you get in your car and tell the truth again. Return your internal commotion to the world. Then the carnival begins, the world dances, joy is about. You are Who you really, really, really are, the Unmoved Mover of the world.

This is not fiction. Set up a video camera in your car, and you will see the world moving. Video cameras don't lie. Come on, you could at least be as truthful as a video camera! If only we dared to look and live in God's world, instead of man's disfigurement of the world! How many of the things that man does to the world are making it into hell! All that commotion invades me, and I lose my peace of mind. All that confrontation invades me, and I lose my love. Everything that takes me from God's world into man's world is sending me into hell.

Now, I'm not saying we don't play the game. From the point

of view of Delta Airlines, I move presently from the Bay Area to Los Angeles. I pay for a ticket, and there are so many miles, and it takes me so long. I play that game. But I keep my serious attention on Who I really, really am, where I never move at all. It makes for safer driving. In England, we have an offence called driving without due care and attention. Well, I say that to pretend the country is still and you are moving is driving without due care and attention, and it is a very bad offence.

The Truth is such fun. It's amusing and refreshing. It's hilarious. And, my God, it's practical!

There are many, many ways Home to the place we never left, but practice is essential. You practice because it is fun, and because it lubricates personal relationships, and because it's full of surprises, and above all because it's being truthful. It's a huge adventure, full of discovery.

The third stage that goes along with the second is *trusting* this. That's the big one. If I put my trust in the little one in the mirror, if I put my trust in Douglas, Douglas will always let me down. It's his nature to let me down. This One never lets me down, not giving me what I want but what I need.

Well, that is my story. I would like to hear now what you have to say.

Question: What is your favorite way of showing people Who they are?
DEH: I get my face about a foot away from theirs, or a little further, and say, pointing to my face, "Look at all this stuff." I get them to look at this beard and so on, and then, while asking them if there's anything to match it where they are, I draw my hands through the air in front of their face and just rub out, ease away, pull to one side the idea they have of that thing there. I stroke it off, you see, left and right, and say, "Are we face to face, or is my face the only one you have at this moment?" I find that

a quick and effective one.

In emergencies, it can be shared in about a minute and a half, or less. People sometimes ask me on airplanes what I'm up to. I say, "I'm lecturing at universities and so on." They say, "What about?" I say, "I haven't got time to explain, but I've got time to show you." It's as easy as winking to show people what one is up to.

Of course, objections come up. Many people want to wriggle out of acknowledging Who they are. Others don't.

Question: How do you stay centered when the face in front of you is angry?
DEH: If you've got a face Here to confront that angry person with, you are terribly vulnerable. You're not safe. But this No-face is the eternal safety. You cannot be destroyed. You cannot even be fundamentally hurt because in Who you are Here is nothing to be destroyed or injured. This is the position of total safety.

Also, when you see that angry person, you see them into your Space. Then you are establishing the asymmetrical pattern instead of the symmetrical one, and there's a chance that the anger will be reduced or even disappear when there is no confrontation.

The experience we've had together this afternoon is about facts, not about feelings. It's the truth that sets us free, not good feelings or positive feelings or kindly feelings. Our feelings are like the weather, always up and down. We're always trying to adjust our feelings and get them right. If we just leave them on one side while we attend to the facts, then our feelings are going to benefit a little, perhaps a lot. Well, you might say that if we're truly enlightened, we will never have bad feelings. Oh really? Someone says to Ramana Maharshi in *The Talks*, "Master, you're

a great sage. You never have bad feelings. You never have ego-
tistical feelings." He replies, "That's wrong, rubbish. In the Sage,
the ego rises again and again, but he recognizes it for what it is,
and it doesn't do him harm." Bad feelings will come up. Then
you're Space for the bad feelings. As it's face to Space, so it's bad
feeling to No-feeling, to the absence of feeling. Asymmetry is
the name of the game. All these bad feelings and negative things
are opportunities for coming back to the place which is free of
everything you can name.

What we're on about today is not a marvelous peak experience *à la* Maslow. It's a valley experience, which we can always
have. Who we are is available whatever our mood: when we're
angry, when we're confronted by a nasty person, when we're
joyful. This Space is always available. That's why I say it's the
truth that sets us free, not feelings. But if we stay in the truth,
then some of the perfume of Who we really, really, really are will
rub off on the feelings we have, and that will help us and the
world quite a bit.

Question: Can you say more about seeing Who you are and love?
DEH: You want to love well the one you love. There's only one
way truly to love that person. It is to disappear in his or her
favor. We are built to give our lives for one another. This is an
exquisite design for living, that we give our lives for one another.

I look at my young friend next to me here. The only way that
I can receive his face is to die as Douglas and be resurrected as
him. I guess it is the same for him. He gives his life for Douglas;
I give my life for him. We are disappearing in each other's favor.
We are built for loving. I'm not talking about the feeling. I'm
talking about the ground from which love can grow and flourish. Here, I really am in receipt of him, not because I am a nice
person, because I'm not. Douglas is not a very nice person. My

friend is not a perfect person, either. He looks pretty good, but he's not perfect. But he's built for loving.

This disappearance is real disappearance because when I look Here, not a molecule is left, let alone a cell, let alone some goo or chemical stuff—as you saw for yourself when you looked at the Clarity where you are. There's no dust on this clear Window. This is real death. It's a more complete death than the one the mortician deals with because he's left with some mess, something to get rid of. There's *nothing* to get rid of Here. "Greater love hath no man than this, that he give his life for his friend."

We're all like this if we tell the truth. In this sorry world in which there is so much fear and hate and confrontation, the splendid, marvelous truth remains: the fact that the wickedest, the most foolish, the most aggressive people are still built to this pattern—every one of us is. The most "horrible" people are built the way you are built, absolutely.

The most wonderful reminder of what we are on about tonight is to have someone in front of you. It may be someone you love, it may be someone you are having terrible problems with. How do you address those problems? How do you sweeten the atmosphere? How do you reduce the tension? By telling yourself the truth that you are not confronting that person but are busted wide open for that person. Literally busted. It's true, isn't it? You never confronted anyone in your life.

You are always meeting people. You have a responsibility. Shall you tell the truth and make it face to no-face, or shall you lie and make it confrontation? It's a simple responsibility. Shall it be confrontation, or shall it be non-confrontation? There's no third position. And what an enormous difference it makes to a relationship. The fear goes out of it, the embarrassment goes out of it, the fun comes into it. It's not a perfect answer to all our relationship problems. I don't guarantee that when you see Who you are, you will have a perfect domestic scene from then on. I don't say that, but certainly things will be very much changed. It really does make all the difference in life to live from this truth. It's a beautiful, loving, wonderful thing, a superb design for living. Hidden under this show of hate and fear and nonsense, there is this simple, divine truth of giving our lives for each other. "Greater love hath no man than this, that he give his life for his friend." Superb! Don't we need it nowadays!

Can you measure the effect in the world of our seeing this tonight? This is not without its effect, believe you me. When you see the truth, you are doing it for others as much as for yourself because Who is doing it is not an individual. Who is doing it is the One who is the inside story of all these contestants on the face of the earth. You are doing it for the others and as the others as much as for yourself. And if we have a feeling of responsibility and caring for this sorry old world, we start with ourselves because our true self is the Self of all. We are telling the truth for others as others.

Question: I lose sight of being the other person because I am coming from this stuff that runs me inside. It causes me to focus less on the other person and more on my anxieties and fears and needs, and that cuts the other person out, in a sense.

DEH: Yes, but if you really look, you can look past the anxieties and fears to Who you really are, to the Space. To attack our negativity, to try to forget or overlook or deny or get rid of our bad feelings, our fears and doubts, our dislikes and anxieties, probably reinforces them. In spite of the fact there's fear, I can still look past it and see I am not the fear because I am clear of it. I am Space for the fear as I am Space for your face. The fear comes and goes. It is not central. Look, I'm going to Thailand, to a region where every lavatory is said to have its resident spider as big as my fist. Well, where is my fear of the spider? I don't find it Here. The fear adheres to the spider over there. So, I am spiderless Space for that spider, and I'm hoping that in Thailand I shall have an easier time on that account.

Question: I often think of the experiments when I am stuck going round and round in my head. When I'm stuck right here behind my face in my brain, I lie down and do an experiment. Also, sometimes when I lie down in the fresh, green grass and I see the clouds going by, I forget that I am in my head.
DEH: But you aren't in your head!

Question: I am in my brain, but I'm not stuck in there. I am part of everything.
DEH: Well, you're *not* part of everything, dear! You are everything! Look, I'm saying you don't have a brain or a head there where you are but here where I am. (Oh, I'm sorry! You're the authority!) Well, if you insist you have a brain there, I must say OK. But I'm just suggesting you don't have it there where you are. You talk about being behind your face and in your brain. I'm asking you if that is actually the case right now.

Question: Well, sometimes I'm there in my brain.
DEH: Just look! Tell me: is it dark, sticky, wet in there?

Question: I have friends who would agree they are not their bodies, minds, or feelings, but they wouldn't make the leap into being God. They would say they are individual spirits, separate as their bodies are separate. How does one make that leap from being individual to being whole?
DEH: The proposition is really: "Is consciousness divisible? Has God divided it into millions of separate pieces? Is each one of us

equipped with a personal consciousness apart from the others? In other words, do I have an awareness Here which is separate or somehow distinct from yours there, or are they in fact the same?

Question: *Yes, that's the question.*
DEH: Well, it's not much use finding that I am Consciousness if my Consciousness is still separate from yours. I'm still in the dog-house, I'm still having problems, I'm still really separate from you, and that's anguish.

What is the cure of this anguish? How can we be sure that Consciousness is indivisible? We should *look*. Point again to the place where you are. Have a look at it, and be your own authority.

Notice what your finger is pointing at. I suggest, first of all, that what it is pointing at has no boundaries. It's enormous. It is infinite. Secondly, it has no limiting characteristics. All the limiting characteristics are the other side of your finger, out there in the world. Above all, it has no label on it to identify it as Douglas's consciousness or yours. This Consciousness is impersonal. It has no marks to associate it with me, the little Douglas. And it's aware enough and big enough and alert enough and general enough and impersonal enough to do for the whole world. When I look Here, I don't find the inside story of Douglas. Douglas was left behind out there. Here I find the inside story of everyone.

It may not convince your friends, but never mind about your friends. Keep coming back to the *I am*. These puzzles will solve themselves, not so much intellectually but at a profounder level. I don't say that every metaphysical answer, every theological answer, is immediately given. But if we keep coming back to Who we really, really are, answers will probably be so given that the questions don't arise any more. No longer is there a question to answer when we are firmly established in Who we really, really are.

It is part of the relief from being the little one to notice that there isn't Here a personal briefcase or cabinet of Consciousness separate from yours over there. No, the Consciousness Here is the same in all beings. Of course, this is what all the best mystics have said, talking not so much from philosophical investigation as personal experience. God is all of God in me. This makes sense because God surely is not divisible like a Cheshire cheese. You can't cut God up into little portions like a smorgasbord. God is indivisible. This is so marvelous because it means the whole of God is where you are—not your little bit of God, but the whole of God. If we resist this, it's because we are resisting our splendor, our greatness. The wonderful proposition of all the mystics that I know and would care to call real mystics is that the heart of you, the reality of your life, the reality of your being, your real self is the whole of God—not a little bit of that fire but the whole fire. That's why I'm dubious about the dear Quakers when they say, "That of God in every man." It's not quite right. The great Quakers wouldn't say that. I don't find here Douglas's bit of God. I find the whole of Him.

Question: I am impressed by how concrete the experiments are.
DEH: Yes. The experience of Who you are is incredibly concrete. It's not abstract, vague, spiritual waffle, an unearthly ballet of pale abstractions. It's something really alive, colorful, and dramatic. That seems to me to be very important because it becomes credible then, inescapable. The other way—working oneself up into a mood or into a slightly euphoric, spiritual haze—is not conviction. It is a perversion of real spirituality. True spirituality has got a very special precision. It's got an exactness: looking to see, using the empirical method, believing nothing, doubting

everything.

What is basic about our experiments is that what they reveal isn't religious. It isn't even proto-religious. It is just scientific fact about the Subject, just as ordinary science is scientific fact about the object. It's the same spirit, but the direction is a 180-degree turn. You're applying the same disciplines Here as you do there.

Now, in doing the experiments, we're rather fast to go on from the foundation to the superstructure. Too fast, maybe. We start by saying, "How many faces are there in the bag?" and then we go on to say we're built for loving. The built-for-loving bit is superstructure. Then people can say, "Yes, but . . ." They can argue about the superstructure, and some will say, "I don't like this or that part of it." But foundation stuff is different. Let's go for the foundation. And let's be aware of the difference between what is superstructure and what is foundation. This is a breakthrough for me. In my own case, I had failed to distinguish clearly enough these two levels. Now, I don't go round with my tail between my legs saying of the foundation stuff that there are many ways to find it or versions of it and that ours is only one of them. Let's be uncompromising about the foundations.

Look, when I talk about foundation stuff, I'm not asking for your approval. I'm saying this is the case, take it or leave it. It *is* the case, whether it's recognized or not, whether you're a theologian or a mystic or an artist or a scientist. But when we are talking about the superstructure, we all have different approaches, and there are many ways of looking at things there.

Question: Can you explain the difference between seeing what you see and what you are told to see?
DEH: Only with the utmost difficulty do I see what I see. Like everyone else, I've been brought up to see what I'm told I see, what I think I see, what society and language request that I see.

And seeing the world I am told to see is seeing a fairly crummy old scene, on the whole. To see what I genuinely see from Who I genuinely am is a wonderful challenge and opportunity and reveals the most astounding blessings. When I see what I really see, my gosh, it's a better world. And this isn't an achievement of some state of mind or spirituality. It is just the innocent eye being open to what is given.

Let me give you a trivial example of how we see what we think we see. We take our feet to be about as big as our hands. Would you do a tiny experiment with me now? Look at your feet, shut one eye, and hold your finger out at about nine inches from where you are. You will find that your finger is at least as big as your foot. My finger is covering my shoe. We don't usually see that, do we? We don't see distant things as small things. We see them as puffed up, inflated. It's just a little example of the surprises lurking.

It's very, very important to come to our senses. I think I see you face to face, and that gets me in deep, deep trouble in my life. My life is in shambles because it's built on confrontation. That's man's world, and it's a miserable world. Now I see what I see: I can see I am open to you. Now that is God's world, the real world, which is full of blessings. Seeing what we see is seeing into a better world. Ultimately, I think it's being in heaven. Being in hell is seeing what we are told to see, what we think we see, what we fear we see.

CHAPTER TWO
Workshop II

Today we are going to take a fresh look at our identity, at Who we really are. I will explain how we are going to do it a little later on. But we must first address the issue of *why*. Why should you bother to look at Who you are? Well, I can only tell you my reasons for looking. Perhaps you will find they are similar to yours.

The first reason why I am interested in my identity is that I have happened. I have occurred, and I needn't have occurred. I could have missed the bus of existence. Do you remember all those spermatozoa rushing to the ovum? I won't go into the biological details, but I turned out to be "me" on account of one particular spermatozoon making it ahead of the others. Now that was a chance in a million, for a start.

The thing which we least value and which is indeed the most precious is the gift of existence. We've occurred! We may be thankful for being American. We may be thankful for being Californian. We may be thankful for being a woman or a man. We can be thankful for a million things. But how many people are thankful for *being*—not being this or that but just being? It's something not only to be thankful for but to be amazed at. I've happened! I'm jolly well not going to die without having a look at what's alive, at what's occurred into my chair, into my pants, while there's an opportunity to have a look at it.

What's occurred into your clothes? What is it? Have a look at it! Don't take anyone's word for it, and don't take Douglas's word for it. You are the sole authority on it. When we join the human club, what intimidation we suffer! We take everyone's word about what has happened except our own. The dying words of the Buddha were, "Betake yourselves to no outside refuge." That's sound advice, but it is taken by how many? You've occurred, and it's beneath your dignity, I propose, to live and die without having a look at who is living and dying. You have a chance to look at it. We're going to take that chance this evening. Point one.

Second, a most extraordinary proposition, an unbelievable, unthinkable, shocking proposition has been advertised down the ages by very wonderful and great people who have survived in the species' consciousness. The proposition is that sitting in your chair at this moment is something of just inexpressible wonder and astonishment and splendor and grandeur—namely, nothing less than the Source and Origin of the whole world. The great mystics have said that nearer to us than all else, the heart of our heart, the soul of our soul, our essence, our salvation, our eternal bliss, is none other than God; that Who we really are is Being

Chapter Two

itself, Reality, Atman-Brahman, Buddha-nature, the Void, Allah, the Holy Spirit, the Kingdom of Heaven, the one Light that lights every man. That nearer to me than Douglas Edison Harding is where Douglas Edison Harding and the whole world comes from. That's wild! Our hair should stand on end. I mean, fancy these little creatures, being born and dying, having every kind of handicap and misery and problem, turning out to be the Origin and Substance and Reality behind the world! What a proposition! Of course, it's true that in some of the religions, some of the time, you got barbecued or crucified or otherwise incommoded for pointing this out. All the same, you can find it lurking there in all the great religions.

Since the great ones of our species have said you are at Center the Origin of the world, and the great scriptures of the world have said you are at Center the Origin of the world, it's irresponsible not to test this proposition, isn't it? It's irresponsible to go through life without seeing whether they had got it wrong or were kidding us. If they were kidding us, let's junk the whole ridiculous notion. If it's true, let's enjoy it. Just because they said it doesn't mean it's true. We are going to test it. We're not going to believe it. We're saying they might be wrong. They may be a lot of con artists, these "great" ones down the ages. All these scriptures of the world may be a big confidence trick. It's for us to test what they say. It's for me to test whether nearer to me than Douglas is the origin of Douglas and everything else. We are going to test these propositions tonight. It's certainly worth spending two hours of our valuable time checking up whether those guys got it right, isn't it?

So that's what we're up to. The first motive is that I'll be damned if I'm going to die before I've really bothered to look at Who is living. And the second motive is this wild rumor that's been around about me and you personally, and I want to check it out.

The third motive I have for looking at Who I really am is that Douglas Harding is troublesome and in trouble. Being Douglas Harding, being this tiny bit of the world, is a dreadful problem. He's just a little guy, one of thousands of millions on the earth, so brief. He's up against all the others, at loggerheads with them, separate, lonely, and afraid. Being what you see—hairy and pink and English and old—is being separate. And being a separate, one-off, temporary specimen of *Homo sapiens*, so-called, is, for me, hell. I promise you, it is just hell. You may find that being a human being works all right for you for the moment. But even if it's working fairly well now, there are times when it doesn't work that well, I suspect. You would be unwise to count on it.

How can the barriers come down between us? How can we really set the scene for loving one another? How can we deeply enjoy one another without fear? How can we come together? Well, there are those down the ages who have told us that when we see Who we are, we will find that the barriers are down and the love is there, not because we've engineered it, not because we've achieved it, but because by our very nature it's there when we see how we are already constituted.

Another reason I am encouraged to look at Who I am is that some of these wonderful people said that Who you are is the most obvious and accessible reality in the world. Mind you, a lot of other people have said it's the most difficult thing to see; you have to go to the East, to the other end of the world, you have to wear funny robes, you can only learn about it from people with different-colored skins and speaking foreign languages. There are a hundred things you have to do, and it's highly inaccessible and difficult. You have to be very, very good and very earnest and very determined to find it, and even then it's difficult, and you perhaps won't find it in this life at all. You may have to go through many lifetimes to find it.

Now, that may well be true for you, if you think it's true for you. But I am lazy, yet at the same time I really want it. Two people come along. One says it's difficult to see and I have to pay this very high price. The other says it's the easiest, simplest, and most obvious thing to see. I'll go for the last guy. I'll have a go and see if he isn't right. And in California, I think you'll go for that guy, won't you? My reading of true Americans is that you go for the guy who says, "I'll show you how to do it now." So, I'm a true Californian here! I'll have a go with the chap who says it's available now.

You say, "Yes, but has this guy who says it's easy got any status?" Well, there's one person who has really encouraged me here: Ramana Maharshi of Tiruvannamalai in India, who died about forty years ago. This great Indian teacher, acknowledged by Zen people and by yogis, acknowledged by millions of people in India as one of the great mystical teachers of this century, said that liberation, which is seeing Who you really are, not what you are told you are, is the *easiest* thing in the world. Of course, just because he said that doesn't make it true, but it encourages us to see by experimentation whether he was right. I mention him for our encouragement.

Now what a contrast! One guy's telling me it's the most difficult thing. The other guy's telling me it's the easiest. I don't find too many middle-of-the-road ones. Ramana says it is the most obvious. He says if *you* can't see Who you are, who the hell can? And surely it's got to be available if I *am* it. At least, it seems to me there's a very good chance that it's available. And I would suggest to you that if you say he's wrong and that it is very difficult and that you are on the road and that one day you hope to see Who you are, I suggest that you don't want to see Who you are at all. What you like is being on the road and, for some reason best known to yourself, which I respect, you don't want liberation yet. You are like the young St. Augustine, who had that wonderful prayer: "Oh Lord, make me chaste, but not yet!"

I'm perhaps treading on some corns here. I think it's OK not to want it now. It's OK to get a lot of mileage out of this adventure. But I'm impatient, and you may be impatient like me. I'm not one of those people who are going to take their time over it, perhaps several years, perhaps all their lives, perhaps fifteen or a hundred lifetimes. Of course when, after putting in all that work and meditation and seriousness, the realization finally strikes you, you probably will have a peak experience. But if you're like me and impatient and you want it now and you see it now, you are unlikely to have a peak experience. You'll probably say, "Yes, yes, now what next?"

Ramana says that it's the most available thing, that it's the most obvious thing, that seeing Who you are is easier than seeing a gooseberry in the palm of your hand. Most of the people around him said, "Oh, what a marvelous, dear master he is! He can do it, but none of us can do it." They worshipped him and adored him and never listened to what he said. "Oh, the pity, the pity," he said. It's strange. We think we want to see Who we are; we think we want to be free. But in all of us I perceive a great resistance. This resistance to seeing Who we are is largely due to the fact that seeing we are nothing seems to be the end of the story. If we can quickly go on to perceive that as nothing we are also all things, that it's a case of trading one little guy for the whole world, then we can see it's very good business. It's not losing out. Quite the contrary. But the threat seems to persist.

Now, Ramana and company are very insistent that it's available at this moment just as you are, without further discipline, without further meditation, without further accomplishment of anything. Ummon, a Japanese master of the twelfth century who is very well regarded, said something like this: "It would seem good sense to get rid of your bad karma so as to clear the way to enlightenment. The problem is that it doesn't work too well." He said the way of Zen is first to see Who you are and to get rid of your bad karma afterwards. For my money, seeing Who I am is so easy and so obvious, while getting rid of my bad karma is a big deal. I wouldn't know how to go about the latter at all, but I find that seeing Who I am is the easy thing, and that I will do first.

So, here's Ummon encouraging us, saying, "First see Who you are. Get your enlightenment first, and deserve it afterwards." Well, that suits me. It's rather like buying a television set. We take delivery of the darned thing and enjoy the programs, or suffer from the programs, from the very beginning, but then we pay over the months—on the never never, as we describe it in England. In the case of seeing Who you are, however, you take delivery of your television set, and the payment is the viewing. That's good business. However rotten your karma—I'm not an expert in the field—but however rotten your karma (and it couldn't be much worse than mine, I guess), I don't see any reason why it should stand in the way of what we are going to have a look at presently.

Wittgenstein, the philosopher, says the things that are most essential for our lives are all of them hidden by their own obviousness. True. There are two traditions concerning how the Buddha felt about sharing the experience he had under the Bo tree six hundred years before Christ. The normal tradition is that he thought it was going to be terribly difficult to share this vision with others because they might not be prepared to go to the lengths of asceticism he had been to. So he devised the Eightfold Noble Path and the *Sangha* in the hope that at least a few monks and nuns would see Who they were. But there is an alternative tradition, associated with Tibet and Burma, in which the Buddha said that it was going to be terribly difficult to share this vision of reality for a different reason. Why? Because it was so obvious, people would never believe it.

To summarize so far: I am going to look at Who I am because I want to see Who is alive while I'm alive to see, I want to find out if this rumor about being the Origin of the world is true, and I want to escape the hell of separateness. And I am encouraged by the claim that seeing Who I am is easy and available now.

The fifth reason for investigating Who I am is that I live in a culture which is based on the scientific attitude, and I have the scientific attitude. If we look at the history of science, what do we find to be the precondition of the scientific attitude and of scientific achievement and discovery? The precondition is that you look and you doubt everything you can doubt. In medieval times, science was very handicapped. It never really got off its launching pad. Why? Because people didn't experiment and see what happened. They looked up answers in the Bible or in Aristotle. For example, if they wanted to know whether a big stone fell faster than a little stone, they looked in Aristotle. But then along came Galileo, who went out and got a couple of different-size stones, carried them to the top of the Leaning Tower of Pisa, and subjected the whole question of which fell faster to the test of direct, naive experience. He found, of course, that they both fell together and arrived together at the bottom. He got into terrible trouble with the Church over this. Soon people were discovering all sorts of things, and they had to be very careful how they published their discoveries. Otherwise, they could find themselves in deep trouble and even burned at the stake, which Bruno was, for example.

So, our culture is founded on seeing what we see instead of what we're told to see. It is based on humility before the evidence. I do not want to look up Who I am in a book. I am going to look for myself.

What I've done, then, is to give you some reasons for looking at Who and what we are. Now we are going to test scientifically this proposition which the sages throughout history have put forward: that Who you really are is not a bit of the world but is the Reality behind the world. We have a number of experiments. You don't have to like all of them. You don't have to understand them. I don't understand any of them. But any one of these will take you right Home to Who you are. And the simpler they are, the better. However, whatever you do, don't believe a thing Douglas says. Test it.

The first experiment is about what you are looking out of. It is a simple one called the Spectacles, for use in ordinary life.

You seem to me to be looking out of two little holes in a meatball—two tiny, weeny peepholes in a meatball. Is it true for you where you are now? How many eyes are you looking out of? Those who have spectacles, hold them out in front of you. And those who aren't equipped with them, make a pair with your fingers at arm's length. Look at those two windows.

Will you slowly, with great attention, please put them on, and see what happens as they get nearer and nearer? Bring them right up, and when you have put them on, put your hands down. Is anybody looking out of two little holes in a meatball?

If you went out in San Francisco and asked everyone in the city, "How many eyes are you looking out of in your own experience?", how many would say "Two"? I'd guess about ninety-nine percent. That means we've gone crazy. It means we

43

really are not well. Lying about things out there in the world is not very good, is it? Lying about whether the traffic light is green or red or amber—that's serious, but it's not nearly as serious as lying about what is here at the Center of our life. Here we had better be truthful. And your experience now, I guess, is that you are not looking at me out of two holes in a meatball. Nor is it a small hole that you are looking out of, is it? Isn't it a great big window? Without smiting your neighbor, outline the frame of the window. Isn't it infinite? Actually, it goes on and on forever, and the window has no frame. There's no glass and no frame. You are looking out of infinite Space, and that's what you are at this time at the Center of your life.

In the East they talk about the Third Eye. If this isn't the Third Eye, then I'm not interested. I say this is the true Third Eye, and I suggest you never looked out of anything else than this Third Eye. The Third Eye is available in downtown San Francisco, perhaps more available than it is in Lhasa, or Mexico, or Japan. It's available now and here in this room, isn't it? Did you ever look out of anything else? Is there any dust on the window? There's a teacher who said that if your eye is single, your whole body shall be full of light, having no place dark. That same teacher said that we find the everlasting Kingdom within us, and we find it when we are as honest and simple as little children. Here it is, the Single Eye. That's all we need. We could go home now. Living from our Single Eye, we have the secret.

Of course, we have other points of entry into the place we never left, though the Single Eye is one you can use without drawing attention to yourself. When you are walking down the street, you can be this great big window. Tell the truth.

The next experiment is called The Little One and The Big One. It presents very clearly two versions of ourselves, and it allows us, in fact requires us, to choose between the two. It is a laboratory experiment, and in it you are not only the experimenter but also what is experimented on—so you have a very responsible job. What you decide I shan't quarrel with. It would be impertinent and absurd for me to tell you what to find. I can tell you what I find, and if I seem to be telling you what you should find, you're going to have to forgive me because I'm not expressing myself very well. You're the authority.

The trouble is we've allowed everybody to tell us what we're like. To be a human being is to have succumbed to a confidence trick. The confidence trick is that we are what we look like. I am not what I look like. You've got what I look like; I've got what I am. I've got what you look like; you've got what you are. They're not anything like one another. I'm not what I look like, thank God.

When we do this experiment, it's essential to look at the mirror or the card and not at me. I'm going to do it as if I've never done it before, I promise. I'm starting again. We're all beginning afresh.

Could you very kindly look at what's on show in the mirror (however painful or pleasurable the sight), namely, your face, the little one. We are going to look at it in a different way from the way we usually do, a little more honestly, with a little more openness to what is given. We may notice some things which perhaps we haven't noticed for a long time.

How very far off that little one is, who we say is ourself in the most intimate fashion. It's as though we are holding a coconut out there in the palm of our hand, so far away it is. Also, it seems to have got twisted round, looking *at* us rather than *out from* us. Strange. If I'm looking north, it is looking south. Isn't it a bit odd that I should identify with a distant something that's looking the other way from me? Keep looking at it. See how small it is now, three inches by two inches.

Very, very important: notice that it's a thing. Things have certain characteristics. One of them is that they exclude other things. They shut them out. Look, it's occluding the background. It doesn't let things in. It's got written all over it, "Keep Out! No Admission!" It insists on itself to the exclusion of others, not because it is nasty but because that is its nature.

A second characteristic of things, and perhaps a more important one, is that they perish. That face has been perishing ever since it first appeared there in the mirror. It is sitting in death row, waiting for execution. You could write its birthday underneath the mirror and put a dotted line for the deathday to be filled in by someone else. The sentence has been pronounced; the date of execution has yet to be determined. Now the question is, does that face belong where you are, or does it belong out there? I don't want to be gloomy, but I do want to be realistic, for it's a matter of life and death to get the answer right, to determine whether I am that perisher or not. In my case, its shelf life is running out fast. If I am that, then I've had it. And, my gosh, have I not grown up and lived on the assumption, the doctrine, that I am that? So the question is, on present evidence, is that face out there, or is it really at the near end of my arm?

Let us answer that question by carrying out the first part of the experiment: bring the face in the mirror slowly forward, with great attention. Notice what's happening. As it gets nearer and nearer, the chin disappears, the forehead goes, the nose grows, the eyes get bigger and a little bit hazier as the mirror gets to six inches, and hazier still, and the nose bigger still, as you come to three inches, and to two inches, and at one inch, you've lost almost all of it, and it's very difficult to see anything. Move it to half an inch, to a quarter of an inch, and eventually as far as it will go, and you'll find that your face has gone. You can't put it on. To find it again, you have to send it back to where it was.

There was a poet who asked, "Oh death, where is your sting? Oh grave, where is your victory?" We can answer his question now, after two thousand years, and say, "A few inches away, Paul dear, a few inches away." Death cannot come to me. I have drawn its sting.

Where does that face really belong? You couldn't fit it on your shoulders Here. The poor little thing is loose out there. It needs a body. Well, let's find a body for it. Turn to your neighbor, and put your head on your neighbor's body, where it fits perfectly. This is hilarious, isn't it? I put my mirror face on your body, and you now have a young body and an old face.

Why does your face fit on your neighbor? It fits because it *belongs* to your neighbor. My face belongs to you. We steal our faces from other people and put them here on our own shoulders. This isn't petty larceny; it's grand larceny. Your face does not belong to you. It's not your property. You can't put it on. Give your face to other people. It will fit on everybody except you Here—and yet this is the one place we crazily, under social pressure, put it. The one place I put this thing is the one place it can never be! It's attempted suicide to attempt it. No wonder I have some problems.

When you give your face to others, when you stop worrying

so much about what you look like, you are much more beautiful, I'd say. When people are all the time thinking about what impression they're making, the life goes out of their faces. They get a screwed-up look.

Now I look in the mirror to see who I'm *not*. I look in the mirror and say, thank God I'm not like that—not Here I'm not.

But what are you then? Well, in the card there's an alternative. Let us turn our attention to the hole in the card—to what we call the "big one." We look at the big one and notice that in every respect it's different from the little one. You see there no eyes, no nose, no mouth, no teeth, no complexion. It's absolutely clear of all the stuff the little one has. In fact, nothing whatever is there. The hole is a perfect hole, absolutely empty, speckless, void.

But notice: just because it's so empty, it's also full—full of whatever you care to put in it. Try it out. Move it around. You can put in it the carpet, the people, all 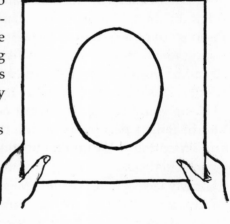 the shapes and colors in the room. The space in the card is so married to the contents that they become the same thing. Because it has nothing of its own, it is potentially all things.

It would be rather marvelous, I think, if we turned out to be the big one instead of the little one. Why? Because the big one is imperishable. We could go out at night and get stars and galaxies in this space, and they would all be perishing, but the space would not perish because there is nothing there to perish. It is empty of itself, the imperishable container of all those perishable objects.

However, at present, it's not quite what the doctor ordered. It's too small—smaller than I care to be—and it's out there, which is not the right place. It's also vaguely human in shape, which is a limitation. A suggestion of mortality lurks there.

Now, we tried to put the little one on, and we failed. We are now going to do the most crucial part of the experiment, which is to try this big one on for clarity, for size, for comfort, like a mask, to see if it fits. Very slowly, put the card on and see what happens. Notice what happens to the edges of the hole. I think you'll find the edges go, there's an explosion, and you have become not only that space, but that space extended to infinity. Have you not become the Light by which you see and nothing else, this light of Awareness? And isn't it immense, without edges, clear, and at the same time full of the world? Nothing is in the way of the world. You are Space for the world.

Take the card off for a moment, and consider further this question of what's perishable or not, the question of our mortality and immortality. We could christen the little one in the mirror "mortality," couldn't we? And we could christen the big one "immortality." Now that same poet who talked about the sting of death and the victory of the grave also said, "This mortal has put on immortality." Isn't that what we just did? Didn't we put on immortality, and didn't it fit like a glove? What happened to mortality when we tried to put on the little one in the mirror? We lost it, didn't we? You can put on immortality with the greatest of ease, but you can't put on mortality. Why? Because, I suggest, where you are is the eternal light of God, which is immortal if anything is. Your mortality is what other people get, it's what you see in the mirror, and it's certainly coming from where you are. But the mortal bit cannot arrive Here at the Center and kill you. It remains out there, while our immortality is

Here. I look in the mirror to see the mortal Douglas. I look Here to see the immortal Origin and Refuge from Douglas. This is a place where I'm let off being Douglas, and this means that I am—we are—imperishable.

Could we try the big one on again, and notice this time whether you can fill the hole with your face or whether you can't—whether the hole remains absolutely empty or not? The edges go, and you are the No-thing, or Emptiness-Fullness. Have you any boundaries now? Aren't you Space for the world to happen in? The little one was a thing, and it perishes. The big one is No-thing and Everything, and it doesn't perish, although all its contents do. You're the authority. I'm not telling you, really. I'm asking you. Aren't you the No-thing which is the Container of all things? Is that not your nature—to be No-thing totally united to all things?

OK, you can take off the card.

The card and mirror are quite useful, versatile tools. What they do is give a résumé of my life. When I came into the world—or rather when the world came into me—I was for others a small baby. However, for myself I was boundless. A baby is Space for the whole world to happen in—a chaotic world, yes, but a wide world. I came in as the Big One. Then, as the years went by, I began to notice a little one there in the mirror. It kept turning up, kept staring at me. It seemed like a rather devoted friend, like a devoted dog—or, as I eventually learned, a devoted Doug!

For all of us, at first, that face in the mirror is not our face. It is our little companion whom we ignore, whom we put up with, whom we play with. A six-year-old girl I know brought home one of those panoramic photographs of the teachers and students at her school. About fifty humans were in the picture, and she named every one perfectly—except one. She didn't know who that little girl was. Who was it? Yes, you're right. It was she.

Chapter Two

When we're that age, or perhaps a little younger, we don't say, "That's me!" when we look in the mirror or at a photograph." We are the Space for that little girl or boy.

Then comes the second stage, in which we are still this immensity, but for social purposes we learn to look in the mirror and say, "Yes, that's me"—especially when we're naughty, under criticism, having to behave ourselves, learning good manners at the table, or having a rather rough time. Parents and siblings and so on keep saying to us, "That's you." I bought into that. I agreed that was me, Douglas, in the mirror. And then the me crept from the mirror up my arm to Here. At the same age, however, when we're cheerful and in our natural state, at ease, not under criticism, we're still the Big One, absolutely busted wide open, not bounded by that face. That's a happy, blessed time—from four, five, six years old to perhaps ten, even twelve. It varies a great deal. You have joined the human club, but you haven't paid the whole subscription.

What is the whole subscription? It is the third stage, and it is incredible, absolutely incredible. It can start off by being the great thing, but it becomes crazy and hell. What is this third stage? It is this: we blank out the Big One as if it never existed. It's incredible. We edit out the Space and become our face. We become the little one. We shrink from being as wide as the wide world to being what we look like. This is what happens to the growing child. Is it any wonder that teenagers are furious and angry without knowing why? The reason is that they have shrunk from being as wide as the world to being just the little one in the mirror. They've lost their immensity.

It's a stage we all have to go through, and it's hell. Because I've blanked out my Capacity, I'm up against the world. I confront the world. I've got a thing Here which is blocking my Space. I've got a block Here, a block in two senses. I become a perisher, because the little one is dying. It's hell. And it's untrue; it's all imaginary. Hell is the product of a very, very powerful, very vivid and disordered imagination. It is a misunderstanding, a social fiction, but, gosh, it is so real in another sense. Please God, let us not have to stay in this stage too long. So that is the third, tragic stage: I am what I look like.

The fourth stage, which we have arrived at by virtue of this experiment, is a perfectly simple, obvious thing. What is it? It is the Immensity here. We never left it, really. The third stage was a dream, a nightmare. What I've seen by putting the big one on is what I am for myself—boundless, capacious, imperishable, busted wide open, speckless, and awake. That's what I am Here. The face in the mirror is what I look like there. And the distance between them is about a meter.

So there are the four stages. The infant, who is as wide as the world, without boundaries. The child, who is also like that, but for social purposes has agreed to shrinkage into that little creature, playing a double game. The adult, who becomes that little one. And the seer, the Big One who is awake Here.

One final thing I want to say about this experiment, which I think is perhaps one of the best things. What is our heart's anguish, what is our problem in life, what is our sadness? It is loneliness, separation, and alienation. There in the mirror we are separate. There, I am Douglas. There, you are you and he is he and she is she. But Here I am you. I say to everyone in the whole world, Here I am you. And that is healing. I know no healing but the healing which enables me to say, Here I am you. To say I am just the little one is to be sick. This is our healing: Here I am you. And it is the ground of love, and the ground of sanity, and, I guarantee, the ground of everlastingness. End of experiment.

Questions?

Chapter Two

Question: *How would you share this idea with people who, because of disfigurement, are constantly being reminded by the world of what they look like?*

DEH: I take your point, but I find that many normal-looking people go through a period when they are hugely distressed about their looks. Therefore, I wouldn't regard a person handicapped in that way as a special case. We all go through some kind of hell or another.

Take the case of an eighteen-year-old girl who came to one of my workshops. During the workshop, she didn't get the point of Who she was because she was so disturbed. She came to me the next day, and she still didn't get the point. She was thinking of committing suicide and just wanted to get my view on it, or at least some relief or refuge, or perhaps she was wondering whether I could change her decision. We sat on a hill overlooking a wide river, and I asked her, "Why are you so depressed and angry, sad to the extent of wanting to kill yourself?" And she said, "Because I look terrible. I think my appearance is disgusting." She was averagely good looking, and she was intelligent. It was no good telling her that in my experience she was quite a good-looking girl. You know what was wrong with her? It wasn't her face. It wasn't her looks. There was nothing wrong with her face. It was where she put her face. So I said, "Where's your face at this time? I have your face Here, and you've got Douglas's face." I felt like I was Doctor Harding, giving her a painless facelift of three feet. It saved her life. She went back to school, and I was told later that there was extraordinary change in her, that her life had normalized.

Now, you may say that it could be even worse with someone who was hideous. I don't think it could have been worse. It was very, very bad. I think many of us go through this stage. The question is our identity. The little guy in the mirror whom I look like is a part of the universe, and it's perishing. Of course, in reality it's absolutely fine that it's perishing because the one Here is not like that at all and does not perish. I'm not what I look like. I must distinguish between the perishable piece of me, which is the face and all the stuff out there, and my eternal nature Here, which is imperishable. However, this girl had put the little one that was perishable onto the Big One, where it didn't belong, and the block and the misery were driving her to madness and suicide. When she saw it off to where it belonged, she was herself again.

If you are dealing with a disfigured person, first of all, don't be so sure that they are worse at seeing Who they are than you are. I'm not so sure about that. They have a very great motive for looking Here. I don't think because we see them the way we do that they are stuck in a body more than we are. I would say there are two things to do when you are dealing with a person like that. First, mind your own business and be Who you are, see Who you are, live from your Space, and you will put It across to that person even without talking about It. Your love, your openness will help so much. And secondly, why, if it's appropriate, you could do the kind of thing that we've done here today. Just point out that the face in the mirror and all that stuff she sees down here, her arms and legs, are peripheral to her. They are what other people are getting and what she's getting out there, but Here she's absolutely perfect as Who she really, really is. You can show her that. Without fail, you can show her that.

Question: I get the feeling that we are not talking about just the face. We are talking about everything that a person is. All the anger and anguish that we are burdened with is not out there in the face. If you are suicidal, sometimes it's not coming out of your face; it's coming out of burdens in the past.

Chapter Two

DEH: I'm telling you what happened. I'm not arguing about it. What you say is absolutely right, but these troubles, these ideas, these thoughts and feelings, constellate round that face. The face is enormously important. Why is it important? Because it is the key to solving the problem of Who we are. And you see, really, there's just one problem in my life. If I get that right, my life is all right. If I get it wrong, my life is wrong. The question is, "Who am I really?" Who I am really is Who I am Here for myself, and for me it's the Big One. The face is my temporary appearance. It's Douglas, and I'm soon going to be let off being Douglas. Thank God. Enough is enough is enough. But Here I've already been let off being Douglas, and this is Who I really, really, really am. It's the identification with the one that's temporary and mortal and out there, taking that one and putting it Here, which is my sorrow, which is at the root of my psychological problems. So the face is enormously important because all this stuff constellates around it.

But you may still insist, "Here I have a mind with thoughts and feelings, which is the real problem, not my face." Well, we have an experiment about that. We could make it our last experiment. Could we do it rather than talk about it? This is really research into Who and What we are, and I recommend to you this investigation.

You see, we all assume we are that little one. I say you are not that little one. That little one is your temporary appearance, and your eternal reality is the Big One. After having seen the Big One, we go on confusing the two. They get mixed up in our minds, and it is this confusion which is our problem. We keep going from one to the other, and go on talking just as though we were the little one. That girl's problem that led her to near-suicide was that she had mistaken the little one for herself. This last experiment is to sort out which we really are without benefit of vision and without benefit of identification with the face.

Another way of putting the purpose of this experiment is to find out what you need in order to be yourself. When you buy a car, you get a basic model for which you pay a basic price, and then you have optional extras, like leather upholstery. Well, we're going to look at what is your essential, basic nature, not your optional extras. It amounts to this: what do you need to be you? How much do you need to be your authentic self? Do you need countless things, fifteen things, three things, two things, or just one thing?

Now most objects, in order to be themselves, need quite a few parts to be complete. This chair I've been sitting on needs three things to be a chair. It needs legs or a pedestal of some kind to raise it off the ground, it needs a seat, and it needs a back. If it didn't have a back, it wouldn't be a chair; it would be a stool. A house needs about four things. It needs a roof, it needs walls, it needs a floor, and it needs a door. It doesn't have to have a window. It's useful to have a window, but I don't think igloos have windows. So, what do you need to be yourself? If you find out what you need to be yourself, you know Who you are. If you find out what you can lose without real loss, without a sense of deprivation, without anger, without distress, without damage, what remains is you.

This last experiment, therefore, is a test we are going to subject ourselves to, an investigation of what is *given* when we drop, as far as we are able, memory and belief and wishes and imagination. We are going to investigate what is left when we close our eyes and tell ourselves the truth about what we find on our chairs right now. You are the authority. On this hangs your life and your death.

Will you please close your eyes and keep them closed? [*Reader: please get someone to read the following to you slowly.*]

Chapter Two

The first question is, where are your boundaries now? Do you have boundaries, on present evidence? What is your shape at this time? Do you have a surface where you stop and your environment begins? What is the shape of that surface, that envelope which contains you? What envelope, what surface, on present evidence?

Do you have *any* shape now, let alone a human shape? How do you know I'm not a wonderful magician that's turned you into an animal? Magicians are always turning people into mice or something. How do you know I haven't done that? Perhaps I have. When we were very little, we played the game of being a railway engine or an airplane or a cloud. All sorts of things we could turn ourselves into very easily when we were very little. Why? Because we knew that for ourselves we had no shape at all. We could be any shape we liked, and we had fun.

Count your toes now without moving them. Toes? What toes? Or your legs, for that matter? Do you have, on present evidence, any shape at all, let alone a human shape? If we really tried hard, couldn't we make ourselves globular or pyramidal, make ourselves into a tree, if we used our imaginations. Isn't it imagination which makes a human body Here at this moment?

Are you a thing in a great big environment, or are you Space or Room or infinite Capacity? Well, is it infinite? Can you find any boundaries to the environment, let alone to this nonexistent nuclear object in it?

How tall are you, on present evidence? Someone asked a Zen master how tall he was. He replied that he wasn't quite sure but he thought he was about thirty feet. I think he underestimated it. Don't you go on and on and on, upwards, sideways, downwards, frontways, backways? Is there any limit to you, and is there anything in the middle, any central object in this vast, vast, limitless Capacity which you are? You are the authority.

Another name for this Capacity is Silence. Are you not now the Silence into which these sounds are dropping? The sounds come and go. Everything that changes dies. Sounds are born into your Silence and die out of it. Silence itself—what can die there? Are you not Silence for sounds, just as you are now infinite Space, Capacity, for all sorts of sensations, like warmths, one or two little tensions, a sense of pressure somewhere? Lots of sensations. And they are all coming and going, aren't they? But are you coming and going?

Then, of course, in this Space, in this Capacity, arising all the time is a great succession of thoughts, of images and ideas, clothed with feeling, arising here in the Space, flourishing, disappearing. Thoughts and feelings are born, flourish, and die in the awareness, the awakeness, of this great Space. Is there anything Here to perish? Isn't it like being an infinite television screen on which the program is sometimes tragic, sometimes comic, sometimes rough, sometimes mild. Shoot-ups, burnings are all going on without effect on the screen. You don't have to clean up or repair it after a wild West program. Isn't this what you are like, this immaculate, infinite Screen? What are you now but this awake, invulnerable Capacity?

On present evidence, what nationality are you? What is your name, occupation, qualifications, on present evidence? Is there anything that survives here and now from those regions, the region of your address and telephone number and nationality, to tell you Who you are? On present evidence, how old are you? Does age have any meaning now? On present evidence, what sex are you? Can you find anything at all, any of those characteristics with which you had identified so strongly? We build that little one up, spend our lives building a picture of who we are as human beings. We must do that. It's not a naughty thing to do. It's a good thing to do. But the question is, where is it? Isn't it out there in your imagination? Is it Who you really are at the Center of your life? Isn't all that stuff peripheral and not given Here and not given Now? In other words, all that self-image which we had accumulated is not oneself. Who are you at this time on present evidence? What can you say?

The chair needed three things to be a chair, the stool needed two things to be a stool, and the house needed four things to be a house. What do you need now to be yourself? Do you need any of that accumulated stuff to be yourself? If you needed it, wouldn't you feel discomforted now? Wouldn't you feel you had been robbed? How do you feel? How does it feel to be stripped of everything you had identified with, that you had spent so much energy and enthusiasm building up Here, this personality, these achievements, these qualifications? How does it feel to be peeled of that stuff, to lose sight of it, to let it go, to have it taken away from you? Do you feel angry, disgusted, insulted? Do you feel you have come to a strange, dangerous, horrible place where you don't belong? Or do you feel that you have dropped many, many burdens, all burdens really, falling like leaves from a tree with such ease and with such readiness, and that you have come Home to the place where at last you are unburdened of all things, the place which is your bedrock and your eternal home? Because if you feel that, I would say that you are awake to Who you are.

I put it to you that you are not, in fact, able on present evidence to say what you are, to say, "I am this" or "I am that," giving answers such as nationality and name and age and sex and humanness and all those other things. If you could, it would be the death of you because all that stuff dies. Like the morning dew, it perishes. But it's impossible now to find any of those things. What can you say? I suggest you can say one thing and one thing only: *I am*. Whose name is that? *I am*. Is that the name of the one who will perish, or is it the name of the only One who will not perish? *I am*: this is your true identity, is it not? Is there a more prestigious, marvelous name to have than that? Do we deserve it? Are we built to that divine design? *I am*, and even beyond *I am*. *I am* is too complicated. You rise, with no help, from the unspeakable, the unknowable, the mystery.

Doesn't it feel absolutely in order, right, true, comfortable? Isn't this entry into our true nature, and haven't we been this all along but we just didn't notice it? Isn't this our Homecoming? You are the authority.

In a moment, we will flood this Space with color and shape. Does your name change from *I am* when you flood the Space with shape and color and movement? I suggest your name will still be *I am*, the name of the One who does not perish. Let us try it now. Open your Single Eye and flood the Window with a wonderful view. Your name remains, I suggest, *I am*.

Question: In this meditation, I didn't experience the security you were talking about. I experienced a lot of anxieties, injuries, discomforts.
DEH: That's a very good comment. You experienced lots of anxiety. Well, exactly. And if we had extended the experiment, I think we would have found in this Space that we experienced with closed eyes all sorts of thoughts and feelings, like anxiety, like hope, like joy, like sadness. The point is that all those things come and go. The thoughts, the feelings, the sensations are a kind of program going on in our Immensity. But if they change—and they do, these feelings, positive and negative, arising from this Space, flourishing in this Space, dissolving in this Space—we are not those feelings. They are a kind of furniture of the Space we are, on loan, ever changing.

We can try and suppress or deal with or improve or think our way out of the difficult thoughts, feelings, people, or whatever is bugging us, or we can cease to resist and just become aware of them from Who we are. Who you are has got unwelcome guests. God has a lot of unwelcome stuff going on. You see, God doesn't like cruelty and misery, boredom and depression. God doesn't like those things. But they were the price of her universe. She likes the positive things; she doesn't like the negative things. But she couldn't make a universe without that contradiction. She just couldn't do it. There are many things God couldn't do, like make silent bangs or black whitewash. So I say, take on board these bad things because it's God's work to take them on board. Be Space for them, be responsible for them and see what happens. When they are accepted, they are not so bad. They are bearable.

Look, just as I find myself Capacity for you, just as I find myself faceless Here for your face, colorless Here for your color, formless Here for your form, so I find myself Space Here, Capacity Here, for anxiety. The anxiety comes; the anxiety goes. I'm not that anxiety. I'm Space for it. This Space, this Capacity for the changing feelings, is always me, always available. So what I'm on about is not a case of feeling. It's a case of fact. I should have said this right at the beginning of the evening. We are not on about feelings. We are on about where they come from, what is upstream of feelings, the facts. It's facts which will bring us relief from our anguish. Feelings will not.

We're always trying to manipulate our feelings. They are up and down like English weather, always changing. The only way to do something about our feelings, perhaps not very much, is to go upstream of feelings, and see Who has them. So feelings, whether negative or positive, are an opportunity for seeing Who we are. It's not symmetry; it's asymmetry. It's feelings to No-feelings. The Space I am is not a feeling Space. It's Capacity for feeling. My Nature always is to be free from what is filling it.

And when you see Who you really, really, really are, you will not find that your feelings are all positive. Well, I don't find that. Feelings are up and down. Douglas is anxious, then he's not anxious, then he's happy, then he's less happy. He's continually changing. That makes life interesting. But Who I am Here is not subject to those variations. Who I really, really am is my blessing, my refuge. Nevertheless, I do think that our feelings are somewhat ameliorated, the anxieties somewhat reduced, when we tell the truth about Who has them.

Question: When you asked us to close our eyes and find a home there, I found emptiness and not home there. I found darkness, emptiness, and mystery, not home.

DEH: When we went on with the experiment, and you were unable to say that you were this or that, but still found that you could say *I am*, was that not something beyond emptiness, like a homecoming?

Question: Well, I recognize that I am. But when I just see the darkness, the blackness, I'm not quite sure that I feel at home.

DEH: I was a bit naughty when I talked about feeling at home. But I'm not sorry I did. I find this last experiment the one people are most agreed on. Here we are coming to the place where we can truly say, "I am you." The barriers are down. That's home, the Home in which we can say, "Look, I have your face. I don't have one of my own. Thank you for your face. Here I am you, I am your Reality, because the Space I see Here, the Emptiness I see Here, the Awareness I have Here, is as much yours as it is mine. It belongs to everybody. It's totally impersonal."

In any case, what we do is stay with the facts. Feelings matter enormously, but what we are doing here this evening is to establish the ground, the soil from which the feelings of home and love and communication can grow. Never mind whether it already feels like home or not. Let's stay with the facts, and then we've got the central part right, the foundation. "Seek ye first the Kingdom, and all these things shall be added."

Question: You say you don't have a head, but you do have a head; I can see it. The point you are making is not whether you have a head or not but where your head is. Is that right?
DEH: Of course I've got a head, and of course I've got eyes. My head is there in the mirror, and it's vital, and around me is my life of that kind. But the Core of my life, the Center of the center of my life, is different. The Core of my life is this Clarity, which is Awareness. I think it's what Rabbi Ben Ezra, a medieval Spanish Rabbi, a very fine spiritual man, means when he says, "God is the soul of my soul."

Now, you may say that what we're on about is blasphemous, that it is pride, to find that where you are is none other than the mystery and majesty behind the universe, the Specialist in Being, as it were. How terrible to identify with that. It is fine to adore that which is supporting my life, but to claim identity with it is terrible.

Well, there's another way to look at it. The real pride is when I say I run a separate little corner shop of Being Here, in addition to and independent of, or quasi-independent of, God, who runs a hypermarket of Being. Real humility says that my being is that Being. Real humility is to see in what and in whom lies my being. "In Him we live and move and have our being." I'll buy that one. You can read this as a kind of pride, but real humility is not claiming Being for the little guy in the mirror. The little one over there is an appearance. It lacks substance. It doesn't stand up to close inspection. But come up to me Here, to the Big One, and you come nearer and nearer to the center of pure Being. So Rabbi

Ben Ezra says that God is the soul of my soul.

And at the same time, this Reality is in a certain sense wholly other than me. That is to say, wholly mysterious and adorable and unknowable and extraordinary, the great Self-originating One from which all comes. This otherness is extremely important, not to be overlooked. I put that in, in case anyone thinks this is pretty blasphemous stuff.

Question: What do you mean by God?
DEH: Well, I'll give you a kind of outline of God or whatever you want to call it. I love the term *God*. I'm an old-fashioned person.

When we are looking for God, what are we expecting? "The pure in heart shall see God." We have that promise. There are medieval theologians who say that only God can be perfectly seen because only God is perfectly simple. God is visible, they say. Some great ones have said that God is the only visible thing, the only visible No-thing, if you wish; all the other things are so complicated, and they take so long to survey and take in, and you don't remember them. I look at my friend there, and I can't see him really because when I look at his hair, his feet are fuzzy. His hair itself is enormously complicated, what with the way the light is falling, the bit of grayness there, and so on. I work down to his eyebrows and his chin, and already his hair is getting a bit fuzzy. By the time I've got to his feet, I've lost his face altogether. I don't really see my friend. I glimpse him. Furthermore, I've only got a front view. What about the back view, what about the side view, what about the inside? We don't see things; we glimpse things. Seeing the world is glimpsing. It's not real seeing at all.

Real seeing is seeing This way, right to where you are. And what shall we see Here? Well, if we are to see God Here and find God Here, we have to know what we are looking for so that we can tell whether those mystics and sages got it right. I would say we are looking for something very specific, not something vague. And I would say that that which we can name God provisionally (or, if we prefer, *Atman-Brahman* or Reality or Essence or even No-thingness—I don't care what you call it) has five characteristics. The first characteristic is that it has no boundaries, no fence round it, no edges; it's absolutely unlimited in all directions. The second characteristic is that it is absolutely clear, clean, empty of contamination. It is utterly simple, totally transparent, empty of everything but itself, empty even of itself, clearer than glass, cloudless, an infinite sky. The third characteristic is that it is also full of the world. Because it's empty, it's full—full of the scene, whatever the scene is, absolutely united with it. The fourth characteristic is that it is awake, it's aware, it's conscious. And the fifth characteristic is that it is right where you are. The only place you will find Her Majesty is nearer to you than everything else. That's her throne-room, her royal palace, right where you are. The Kingdom is within you.

To sum up, there are five characteristics of Her Majesty: she is infinite, empty, full of the world, awake, and right where you are. Now that's a description of God. But doesn't the description also fit you? Isn't that what you found when you put on the big one in the card experiment? Don't you find that you can describe yourself in these terms?

Question: I see that I am light. Is there anything beyond the light?
DEH: The Light I see when I look Here is, as Rumi says, the Light that lights up the light. It's not candle power. It's the light of Awareness. I see nothing beyond that at all. This is where one is coming from. This is Reality. It doesn't lead places. It is the end of the road. And it's a Light that is awake to itself, lighting up the whole world. This is "the Light that lighteth every man that comes

into the world." The lamps are many, but there is only one Light. We are that Light. There's a Christian mystic called Ruysbroek, who says, "I am the light by which I see, and this light is the light of God. I see God with the light of God. I see God with God. I am the light by which I see, and nothing else." And of course it includes the whole world. It doesn't leave anything out. It's not impoverished. It's the Light which lights the whole world and the Light we all are. Here, I am you. So I don't look beyond that Light.

Question: When I meditate, I often have the experience of that which you were pointing to tonight. But what about trust? There is something in me which distrusts this as an experience because it is an experience. It is still me having an experience, and I'm interpreting it a certain way. It feels very nice, but I'm distrustful. I don't know how to reconcile this feeling of distrust. I'm not sure if I'm manufacturing something or holding on to something.
DEH: It's certainly a very pertinent question. The question of trust is something that we really should address ourselves to.

As regards the feeling that this experience of Space or Void or *I am* or *I am not* is perhaps not ultimate or trustworthy because I'm still around doing it—the relief from that doubt is to narrow the investigation down to some things which are so simple and indubitable that it's hard for you to cook the books. I don't look Here to find relief from my ego or to find a meditator who has disappeared. I look Here (I recommend this strongly) to find how many eyes I am looking out of. I look Here for teeth and whiskers. I narrow the investigation down to some very simple, childlike, foundation stuff, and I just don't find a speck of a speck of a speck Here.

I treat this investigation with the simple honesty that I would treat the investigation of a substance in the laboratory. I don't say, "Of course I see in the test tube some blue liquid with sediment in the bottom, but it may not really be blue liquid. You know, I didn't get up on the right side of bed this morning, I've been nasty to my wife, and I'm feeling rather bad about this blue stuff. I'm not sure if I'm in a fit state to investigate this substance." No, what the hell, you just go in and say, "That's blue." Your darn feelings don't matter a damn, do they? The blue is given. And by the same token, in all simplicity, I just don't find anything Here. I don't worry about abstractions like me meditating or the ego or Buddha nature or the Void. I look Here for a patch of skin, for eyes. How many eyes am I looking out of? Or I hold my ears and ask how far it is from one to the other and what is between them. God's ears are out there. We get refuge from these doubts by simplifying the question.

The second thing about trust is that when you move from out there to Here (actually you don't because you always were Here, and it was an illusion that you moved from Here to there in the first place), you begin to trust It. You find out its incredible expertise and know-how. Being This One never lets you down, I'm quite sure, and being the little one always lets you down. Always. What you do from Here doesn't give you what you want; it gives you what you need. My experience, not to be believed but to be tested by you, is that when I am established Here and see This and am living consciously from Here, I have this which can be infinitely trusted. The world and the little one there are totally untrustworthy; this Here is the fountain of reliability. Total reliability. The way it works is that I lose confidence in the little one and observe what the Big One gets up to. Don't believe a word I say. Test It, and I think you'll find It never lets you down.

Question: *There is unity, and yet there are also dichotomies—yin and yang, male and female. How do you put them all together?*

DEH: I find that Douglas, the guy in the mirror, and indeed the world, is divided between good and evil, beauty and ugliness, left and right, male and female. The phenomenal world runs on duality, doesn't it? And rightly so. If you got rid of the duality, the whole thing would collapse. That's the way the world runs, like a battery with two poles. Now, what is the resolution of that duality but the unity that underlies it? I find it Here in Who I am.

There's a further dualism, of course, between the world as a whole there and the Origin of the world Here, a dualism between what we are looking out of and what we are looking at. But it's not real dualism because they come together absolutely. The Space you are is so united with the world, it gets you right out into the world. When you look Here, the Space is not something private, your treasure Here, a safe place apart from the world to take refuge in, away from that horrid, wicked old world. No, it gets you right out and involved totally with the world because there is no separation. You are full of the world. So when people see this truth and start living from it, their involvement with the world becomes total. They are caring. It's their world. Isn't it a marvelous thing?

You see, when I identify with the guy in the mirror, he turns his back on the world. He says, "I've got enough troubles of my own. Keep out." The One you really are never can turn her back on the world. She embraces the world. She is the world. This is not because you are special; you always were this way.

Question: Would you say that this kind of thinking, emphasizing the unity and the interconnectedness of everybody and everything, is the basis of compassion?
DEH: I'm sure that's so, absolutely. However, we are so interested in compassion and love and oneness—rightly so, too—that we overlook their ground, their basis. We don't give those ideals

sufficient concrete expression in our lives because we are denying the fact that we are built that way, built to disappear in others' favor.

*Question: If the whole of creation is Here, what happens to the Biblical
notion of God as wholly other?*
DEH: Ah, this is an enormously important question. The idea
that there is just the immanent God, that God is inside me and
I've taken possession of God, can lead to terrible perversion, using your vision of Who you are to promote the little guy you are
not. That is a terrible possibility. We need to balance that with
the other side of the divine nature. The view of God as transcendent mystery is absolutely essential. It fills one with worship and
wonder. Immanence and transcendence go together. When we
see Who we really, really are, we are in awe of the mystery, the
otherness of the self-creating One. I find it so astounding that
Consciousness comes up from Unconsciousness. God is the Self-
originating One. That fills me with awe and wonder.

Face to No-Face

PART II

Four
Themes

Chapter Three
The Big One
and the
Little One

Question: You sometimes describe the relationship between Who you really are and who you appear to be as a ding-dong. *What do you mean by* ding-dong?

DEH: It's a debate going on between Who I really am and the particular individual I am associated with for the time being. It's a debate going on between God and one of his creations.

Douglas is a build-up, an ersatz. He is a construction; he's what the people out there that are suffering from or enjoying Douglas make of him. He's a valid ingredient of my life. There he is, out there, and he's totally different from this One. He is one pole of my battery; the other pole is Who I really am. The ding-dong between them is the dynamic of my life. It's not a static thing. It's a conversation, a dialogue between that little one and this Big One. That one is the old man; this One is the new man. That one is the man of earth; this One is the heavenly man.

I would say, if you want to be metaphysical about it, that God would love to have created a universe in which there was no old man-new man, evil-good, ugliness-beauty. He would love to have had the light without the shadow. But he just couldn't. The price of a universe was that the light always had the shadow, the beauty the ugliness, the truth the falsity, the up the down, the left the right, the heavenly man the earthly man. The price of a universe is this ding-dong.

It helps me to look at it this way: there's just one Reality, and this one Reality—after endless eons of boredom in which all was perfect, so nothing happened—pretends to be you and me and all the others. It's a very serious game, an extremely costly game. The nature of individuation is that individuals shall stand up for themselves and announce themselves and look after themselves. "I'm all right Jack" is the theme. "Look after number one." This is not a terrible thing. It's the price of the universe that the individual parts of it shall, as it were, pretend to be God. They pretend to be real and self-sufficient and self-contained. It's a mistaken view, but without it there's no story, no universe.

So the universe is founded on this ding-dong, the debate between the individual who is trying to be real and self-sufficient and the One that he really, really is. It takes the form, in one's own case, of the debate between this First Person singular, present tense, Who I really, really am, and the second or third person I pretend to be.

Question: It's more than a debate, isn't it? You write in The Specter in the Lake *about the image invading the First Person.*
DEH: Yes, it's tough. It's warfare. It's more than a debate. But it

isn't about reforming the individual. There's one simple thing that I have to say, and this seems to apply absolutely: the answer to the problem is never at the level of the problem. It's always at the level of the One who has the problem. For example, I find that this chap, Douglas, the specter that Blake is talking about, never gets any better. If I sort him out, I simply get a different form of the old pattern, of the ego-thing. I get a tarted-up version. This can lead to spiritual one-upmanship, which is one of the worst forms of egotism.

Question: What do you say to the objection that the attitude of not trying to reform Douglas is too passive or is a way of avoiding problems?

DEH: Try it and see. It's exactly the opposite. You take extremely seriously what you find. The contrast between the old man and the new man is very vivid. It's not a complacent view at all. It's realizing that the individual cannot be radically reformed. It can be changed, but these changes are just changes; they're not reformation. They're simply altering the tactics of that little one. This is my experience.

Then there is a twist to the story. Other people are likely to come along and say that one has changed a great deal. In so far as real change is possible, this is the way to bring it about: live from the One who doesn't change. So far from being complacent, or approving of Douglas, or escaping from him, it is exactly the opposite. It is the hardest work that can be done on that little one: constant awareness of the Big One.

Question: How does the feeling that you are getting worse in your life as you're getting older, which you mention sometimes, match with the idea that to other people you're changing in a positive way?

DEH: My friends change; I don't. There's a difference between

First Person and third person here. I find that my friends become very beautiful people, and they do change, and very radically. And they change because as far as they're concerned, they don't change. It's a paradox. Everything at this level is paradox. The best way to change Douglas is to acknowledge that I can't do it.

Question: Is this connected for you with the Barrier, which you describe in On Having No Head, *and the Dark Night of the Soul of St. John of the Cross?*

DEH: Very much. It really helps to see that this is orthodox, Pauline Christianity, the Christianity of all the great Christian saints, like St. John of the Cross, and of Eckhart, William Law, and ultimately Jesus himself, who said, "None is good but God." Paul says, "I know that in me, in my flesh, dwelleth no good thing."

All the motives of the little one are suspect. When I go and improve and approve this little one and think that now I've really sorted him out—now he's a different person, his motives are now pure—that is a lovely trick. Then to his already hideous faults, I'm adding self-conceit. Think of disasters in the world. Little Douglas, this detached part of him called the ego, is thankful he's not involved in other people's suffering. He's got enough of his own. "Keep out!" is his message, and he's so pleased when he is avoiding suffering. Protecting himself is his job.

But this One is crucified. This One takes up the suffering. This One is naked and open. This One is compassion itself. Any hurt in the world is One's own hurt.

Question: Do you mean that sometimes feelings, like the feeling of compassion, can be identified as coming from the One?

DEH: Yes. We should have the humility to be a little bit traditional here and realize that for two thousand years great saints have been working at this, and the common feature of their discovery is: "Not I but Christ liveth in me." Paul goes on and on: "I am crucified with Christ." Father Gerard Hughes, author of the book, *God of Surprises*, says, "God calls on us to become Christ." Not Christs, but Christ. When I hold out my arms, I see the pattern of the Crucifixion. We're built to that incredible pattern. Live that, be that, allow yourself to feel that. You will have the little one cropping up all the time, this attempted invasion, and you've got to recognize it for what it is. Back it goes, ditched, reditched, to where it belongs.

Question: When you keep the two distant from each other, do you distance the feelings of self-interest that are identified with the little one, leaving room for you to be and identify with the Big One, which at times has feelings of joy or compassion?

DEH: Yes. Of course, ultimately, the little one is not real. He is a picture. He is not aware. The awareness belongs to the First Person. The awareness is only Here. It's as though part of your Awareness has got split off and imagines itself to be attached to that little one. But this One is Who you really, really are, your true nature.

It is really true that Who you are is the Origin of the world, everywhichway you look at it. Just think! You never moved an inch. You are the unmoved mover of the world. You are timeless. You have no boundaries. And you are omnipresent. Distance is an illusion. All the world is chickenfeed compared to these incredible facts. We don't have a lively apprehension of Who we are. We hedge on it, or we can't be bothered to look and see if it's true. We are not staggered and amazed and bowled over as we should be by our true nature. Once we do look, everything falls into place.

Consequently, all this sorting out of that little Douglas is trivial and petty. You play that game, and of course you support him and his pettiness. Meantime the glory, the extraordinariness of Who you are, is lost on you. Who you really are is staggering. I found a medieval homily in Hughes's book. He says this is the heart and soul of Christianity: "Arise, oh man. Work my hands. Arise. You who were fashioned in my image, arise. Let us go hence, for you in me and I in you, together we are one undivided Person."

The big thing for me, a development over the last few years, is the realization of the Incarnation. To put it very, very simply, if it is true what Tennyson says, what the Koran says, that God is nearer to me than my hands and my feet and my breathing, then God is Here and This is where he lives. This is the temple of the living God, and these hands are not coming out of an organism Here. I see that they're coming out of the Space. Then these hands do a different job. These feet go on the errands of God, and this voice speaks his words. They are the instruments of Who we really, really are. This is a very different organism from the one we see in the mirror and see around us. This is the First Person, and the First Person is totally different from the third person.

It's because we lack the strength and the splendor of our true identity that we encourage and build up these little things there as a kind of diversion from this One. We get engaged and caught up in that pettiness. This is the relief from it. Ramana was very strong on this: "The answer to your problem is to see Who has the problem." It's never at the level of the problem. If you want to work on the problem as effectively as you can, do it by this indirect means.

Question: The indirect means is to be primarily aware of Who you are?
DEH: Yes. In *Vipassana*, maybe seeing Who you are is virtually

there, but it is not fully or consciously there. The suggestion is that if you work on this stuff that you are not, if you're aware of it and you let it pass, it will die down. But it doesn't die down. It just takes different forms. It is always there. It's *samsara*.

Question: Other practices, like therapy, are very much interested in awareness.

DEH: Yes, they are—generally in ignorance of all the evidence about Who we really, really are. What psychotherapist you ever met tells you to sit in your car and watch the behavior of telegraph poles? You don't watch the telegraph poles, you don't look and see whether you have a single Eye, you don't see whether or not you and I are face to face—all these things which are evidence about your true nature, which are given. I say: let's go for the simple things, let's go for the basic things before we get spiritual, before we get religious, before we get psychological, before we get metaphysical, before we get philosophical. Let's see the difference between the tea that goes in Here and the tea that goes in there. Let's wake up to what's going on.

This is basic stuff, and it's all about Who you really, really are. It's quite independent of your third person and all that subtle, psychological stuff. Who you are is revealed by the childlike, simple, almost infantile things. The therapy business is endless. Who ever came out healed from that? A particular symptom is alleviated, and who knows, maybe you get two new ones of a new order, at a higher level, less evident, more spiritualized or sanctified. The debate arises because we are so unconscious of the splendor of the proposition. "The center of the soul is God," says St. John of the Cross. "God's in; I'm out," says Eckhart. Why the hell should I want to make Douglas into some kind of non-Douglas? I want to live from Who I am, and the best I can do for Douglas is to keep him in his place and concentrate on my true nature Here. It's practical. It's energizing.

But this kind of life isn't a piece of cake. This adventure of ours is a real adventure, and what would we want out of life but real adventure? Every good story has dangers and difficulties, seemingly insuperable difficulties calling for immense effort and courage. Don't our hearts respond to this challenge? Do we want everything to be laid on like water out of a faucet? We don't want it to be laid on. There's something in us which welcomes the difficulties and dangers of this adventure. And it is the great adventure, isn't it?

Question: When you live from Who you really are, does the little one fall away and eventually disappear?

DEH: Not in my experience. I can't dispense with the little guy in the mirror. There he is. Nor can I deny that he is what other people make of me. Nor can I deny that I have all sorts of ideas about what is there in the mirror. One's ideas of personality are constellated round that picture. Some people want to dispose of that guy there, but he is enormously valuable. What does that little guy do? Like a magnet, he pulls this face from Here and shows me where I keep it. This is enormously important, indispensable in my life.

One of the greatest instruments of the truth that God is nearer to me than Douglas is the mirror, which takes that Douglas obstruction out of God's way. My mirror is a marvelous, marvelous teacher, more valuable than all the scriptures of the world.

Question: How do you reconcile the selfish motives that we all have with the claim that you are the One who is free and compassionate?

DEH: Take power, for example. Do I in my heart want power over others? It boils down, as always, to a question of identity. Who are we speaking of? I'm absolutely sure that Douglas is the one who wants power over you. He wants to change the world. But as Who I really, really am, the Freedom, I do not want power over others. I think that human thing is used by the One Here, Who does not want power but has a totally different way of working—through compassion, through love, through persuasion.

In us all is this polarity. It's a debate. If I destroyed the pole of the battery that wants power over others and only had the One that didn't want power, there would be no dynamism. A battery with only one pole is not a battery. It's the union-in-diversity of that little human Douglas, who wants power over others, and this One I am, who rejects power wholly and who says, in fact, that wanting power over others is the great trap. It's as though I plead guilty there and not guilty Here. The little guy is an essential part of one's toolkit.

And, in fact, this polarity is a recipe for a real life. We shake our heads and say how naughty we are and how difficult life is. We complain about the battle between illusion and truth, between good and bad, as though it were some awful foul-up. There's something about it that's proper and beautiful too. This ding-dong between little Douglas and Who I really am, between the earthly man and the heavenly man, the old man and the new man, the slave and the aristocrat, is a recipe for living life. The two cannot be separated. They must be very sharply distinguished and placed, but I can't cut the little one off and say it's a wicked, terrible nonsense and, alas, I'm saddled with it for life. It's not like that. We deplore it, but there it is. O happy fault, that insists on the Faultless!

Question: It sounds as if you are saying that Nirvana *and* Samsara *exist for each other.*
DEH: Right. They are two sides of a penny. That's a wonderful Zen intuition, which means that the world is indispensable. It's

marvelous, that. It's not world denying; it's world asserting.

There's a Hindu scripture that says: In darkness are they who only look *that* way into the world of the mind, of psychology, of nature, of the object, but in greater darkness are they who only look *this* way, into the Void. That's very astonishing, isn't it? This double take, the double arrow, the equality between nirvana and samsara—not only the equality but the identity—is essential. I suppose that many of us tend at one time or another to exaggerate this One and say that Seeing Who You Are takes care of everything, and then at another time to put Seeing on hold while we go into matters common-sensibly, psychologically. We are always tending to get a little bit unbalanced. But the formula is this equality, indeed identity. As we saw in the experiment with the hole in the card, the space and the filling are not separate. Because they are totally distinct, they come together in a most marvelous way. Spiritual life at these levels is all paradox. The more one loses oneself, the more one finds oneself. We are not truly human till we are divine, and not divine until we are truly human. And the union between them is something we are always having to come back to. I personally tend to emphasize this One at the expense of that one. But they're together.

Of course, there's a big tradition, a mistaken one, that the body and the world and the senses are all diversions from This, have no relevance to This, are for rejecting and discounting. That view is one of the handicaps of much Indian spirituality.

Question: What is the significance of feeling seen and recognized by other people?
DEH: I think it's enormously important. We are not fully born until we are thoroughly individuated. True seers are very distinct people. Until we see Who we really, really are, we tend to be imitative and not fully individuated, not our own woman or

man until we are Here universal and impersonal. Until I see Who I am, my self-image is built up on the basis of what is currently approved in society. But when I see Who I am, I become, in a certain sense, a more individuated, separated person. One *lives* this, without brooding on it.

Question: The problem I've got is that often, to get my basic needs met, I've got to go to other people. A part of going to other people is I've got to recognize how they are seeing me. If they like me, they might give me what I want. If they don't like me, they won't. Therefore, I've got to tune in to this little self.

DEH: You are absolutely right. The question is, how do you do that? And how do you get on with other people most efficiently? I suggest that the way ultimately to get on with other people is to *forget* about having good relationships with people, *not* to study that and worry about that and agitate yourself about that. It's perfectly obvious to me that you experience Douglas, and I want you to experience a Douglas who is halfway acceptable, of course. But if I keep worrying about what everyone thinks of me, I am in hell. And in hell, personal relationships are at their worst.

The way to get on with people is to be yourself. I've had to face this one a lot recently, as I've been getting negative reactions. Somebody says, "Douglas, I didn't like what you said or what you did." I'm sorry about it, and I'm not sorry. Douglas as a person is the sum total of what other people make of him, including what I imagine they make of him. But the One Here at the Center is free of all that. If I rest in This, I am doing the best I can in the personal relationships department. If I'm true to myself, living from Who I am, I'm not going to be liked universally, I'm sure of that. I'm going to be loathed here and there, but it's the best I can do.

The question is: Does seeing Who I am help or hinder social

relations, practical behavior, earning a living, going out in the world and dealing with difficult people? My experience is that everything I do there in the full light of Who I am Here, simultaneously looking in and out, is better done. I don't care what it is, whether it is cooking vegetables or cleaning the house or designing buildings or writing poetry. Whatever you are doing, don't lose touch with the One Here. You are going to do it more authentically, more efficiently, more convincingly, more enjoyably, from Who you are than from who you aren't. This makes sense. Living from a lie is not practical, is it? Let me live from Who I am. And I am not, not, not Douglas. I am absolutely not Douglas. Incredibly not Douglas, that perisher in the mirror. I'm not putting him down. I'm putting him out, and that's different.

That is my experience. I've found some friends who agree with me. But for God's sake, don't believe a word of it. Test it.

Question: In psychology, we learn the importance of parents reflecting back to children their behavior in the world: you're this, you're that. How does this fit in with the headless way?
DEH: It's important to be very clear about the essentiality of the second stage of our life, when the child is learning that the face in the mirror belongs to himself or herself. This is the secret of our humanity. Our separate individuality is enormously important, and we are not decrying that. The child has to discover itself as unique. It's as though God has given that child or ourselves someone special to look after. We have to make sure that the little one is given a fair share of the good things, is not ripped off, and is taken care of generally. We have to go through the stage of discovering and being responsible for our unique selves.

But if that's the whole of the story, gosh I'm in deep trouble, because that little one separates me from all beings. That face-thing in the mirror is my certificate of loneliness, of meaninglessness, because a world consisting only of things is meaning-less. Love has no place there. Freedom has no place. It's a world where each is celebrating its own separate individuality—a recipe for hell. Hell says, "Keep out! I've got enough problems of my own." The guy in the mirror is the wrong way round. That's why I can't put him on Here. He turns his back to the world. He says, "I've got enough problems of my own, thank you very much." When I identify with that, I'm in effect saying, "I don't want to know your problems."

But Who I really am Here, the First Person, cannot turn his back on the world. He faces the world. This is why we resist our First-Personhood. We have a feeling that to see Who we really are is to take on the suffering of the world—and the joy of the world—what there is of it.

The shame of separation has to give us a hard time before we can thoroughly enjoy relief from it. I think we have all experi-enced the shame of having a face. The German poet Rilke has a story of his own childhood. He was coming into a room at night and trying to creep upstairs and not be seen by the adults who were sitting round the table with a bright light in their midst. They heard him, and they brought him into the circle. He writes: "There I was under the light, with all the shame of having a face. Must I grow up to be like them?" All the shame of having a face. I'm shame-faced when my face is Here. And I'm not shame-faced when my face is there in the mirror and in other people.

Question: I'm aware of my Awareness, and I'm aware that it is Reality, but this little observer is all the time saying that it knows what my face is doing. It's like a pest. I don't know how to get rid of it.
DEH: First of all, is the observer *little*? Awareness seems to me to be always unlimited. It's a boundless observer, and it's aware of itself as such. You are not doing full justice to the observer when

you write it/her/him off as a little guy inhabiting you somehow.

Now, what you are observing is absolutely limited. The object is always limited and conditioned, whatever it is, whether it's a thought, a feeling, or a percept, anything from a star to a shirt button. All your personal stuff is limited stuff. But you are the enormous, boundless Capacity for it. You have to distinguish the TV screen from the program. You are the screen, namely Awareness. You can see it has no boundaries, in all directions. Now on that screen is a wild western or a soap opera, going on all the time. After you've looked at the shootup on the TV, you don't have to repair the screen. You are free. You are uninjured by the program. We all know about the content but overlook the Container.

Only this morning I was reading in my little red book (I call it The Little Red Book of Chairman Douglas). It consists of quotes for my own personal edification. I came across a quote from Ramana Maharshi where he says, "The ego of the sage rises again and again and again, but he recognizes it for what it is, and it doesn't injure him." There it is. It's rising. But I remain Who I am.

CHAPTER FOUR
D e a t h

Question: What happens when we die?
DEH: The ones that are born die. Are you one of that lot?

This is a matter of seriousness, isn't it? The chap I see in the mirror has been perishing for eighty-two years. Every time I look in the mirror, the perisher is a little bit nearer to the grave.

What you look like is perishable. I am in receipt of what you look like, and I regret to have to say that it is perishing. I look round, and I cannot see any permanence in this room. If I go outside and look at the stars, even they are perishing. Galaxies are perishing, let alone the planet, let alone mountains, let alone nations and cities. Every thing perishes. But there is one thing that doesn't perish, and that is the Reality from which the appearances are coming. What's at the center of my life and of your life is not perishing because there is nothing there to perish. There is only Awareness at the center, and Awareness is not biodegradable. It doesn't perish.

Don't believe anything I say. Test what I say. You are the authority.

Now of course, I am the authority at the moment on what you look like. I am in receipt of all your lovely faces. I enjoy those faces. There is a very touching and beautiful thing about their perishability. Faces are more lovable because they come and go. You know those fantastic words of Shakespeare: "Golden lads and lasses must/ Like chimney sweepers come to dust." There is something pathetic and extremely beautiful about the perishability of everything, the "Golden lads and lasses" coming to dust. All of us, as appearances, come to dust.

But is there any dust where you are, to be swept away by the broom of time, or are you at Center imperishable?

I am the sole and final authority on one thing and on one thing only, and that is what is right Here. You are the sole and final authority on what it's like where you are. You have inside information about what is sitting on your chair. I don't. So I am asking you about this thing on which you are the sole authority, which is your Reality, which is what you are looking out of. It's right where you are, totally obvious, totally available. This is not a sacred or peculiar kind of looking. It's simply looking in the right direction. We all look *out* very happily, but we are very bad at turning our attention round 180 degrees and looking *in*, at the place we are coming from. What you are looking out of is not perishable. There is nothing there to perish.

This is No-thing. I'm visibly No-thing, and where there's No-thing, there's no change. And where there's no change, there's no way of registering time. And where there's no way of registering time, time has not a chance. Time can't survive.

That's all theory and intellectual stuff. But we can be very practical. We have some ridiculously obvious experiments about this. For example, when you go to a place, you look and see what the time is. What's the time in the Bay Area? Well, my watch there reads nine thirty-seven. But what's the time Here? I bring my watch up to Here and find that it cannot record time Here. So I tell you what the time is Here: it's timeless. People say, "Come on, you're not as idiotic as that," and they seek to prove me an idiot, naive to an unbelievable extent. I don't think so. This is simple, strong evidence. Damn it all, the watch goes, let alone the time. The whole thing is incredibly, beautifully on display. All we need is given, if only we're simple and direct.

We only have to look and see. There's nothing Here to change. One of the marks of life is motion. Now, I look Here when I'm walking around and driving, and it's absolutely clear to me that Here is not a twinge of motion. Not an inch have I ever moved in my life. I am totally immobile Here. This is stillness. This is the unmoved mover of the world, as Aristotle would say. And where there's no movement, there's no life.

The onion-peeling experiment celebrates this. When you come up to me, you leave the human region behind, you leave the living region behind, you leave the region of color and shape and materiality behind long before you get Here. Come all the way Here, and you leave everything behind. What am I Here? What is Here—this bare awareness of Being emerging from Non-being, the *I am* from the *I am not*—is where life comes from, is where everything comes from. It's a station of great splendor and great humility. Total poverty.

The conclusion of the onion-peeling experiment is that right at the center of the mandala, where I am, is the absence of any thing. The Center is clear and, therefore, free from life and death.

To be more specific, if you come towards me now with full instrumentation, you get a human being because you are at the right distance. Come a little nearer, and you get tissues, which are certainly far from human, then cells, then one big cell, then molecules and atoms and so on. Well, molecules and atoms and so on are not alive. Way out there you leave life and color behind. Eventually you leave predictability and opacity behind, and you come to regions which are very, very empty of data of any kind. Still you are way out from Here. At the point of contact, I vanish altogether because I was a product of distance. I'm at the Center, which is just free of all that stuff.

Life and death are like black and white. The other side of the medal of life is death because without death life is never possible. There wouldn't be standing room on the planet if we weren't all dying as fast as we were being born. To be born is to die.

But who dies? In my mirror, that little guy Douglas has been dying for eighty-two years. He's suffering from a terminal disease called life. Every time I look in the mirror he's older. But Here I can't find a wrinkle, not a trace of age. You say, well, that dying thing in the mirror is really there where you are. So I bring it up Here. It's gone. I can't bring it up Here. It belongs there.

How one can indulge in spiritual clichés! How they are always going sour and stale on one, becoming meaningless! We talk about "Nothingness" and the "Void," and these words trip off the tongue. They don't really mean much. But when I tell myself that I'm not alive, that I never lived, that I'm flattering myself when I think I am going to die—now, that hits me because that's not a cliché. That's a new one. But it's implicit in the view that Here is No-thing and Here is Void.

It's such a joy, isn't it, to come across new ways of putting old things? It's really marvelous. Thrilling discoveries all along.

Tremendous! Startling! It's just so obvious that without a head you are not alive. There's nothing more dramatic. The head is where the business of life is. You cut it off. You haven't got one. It confirms the idea that I'm flattering myself if I think I'm alive. A headless body has got to be a dead body.

There's no problem about death when you've never lived. Things that live die. Things that are born die. The Unborn—think of the implications of that!

Where I'm coming from is upstream of life. It is the source of life, yes, but it is not alive. From Here I look out upon a snail or the daffodil there, let alone you, and, my God, I discover life.

Question: We take for granted that we're living in the world of life and death. Then we see that we're not. What happens to that world? Does it change?
DEH: I think there are two worlds, actually. They are one world, and yet they are two. One is the world seen from the imaginary location of a thing, a person Here viewing it. The world is seen from the point of view of one of the things in it. Then it isn't the world, really, because it's the world minus that thing. It's a spoiled world because it's not all there. You've taken something out, namely yourself. The world seen from an imaginary human viewer is vitiated precisely because it is seen through that human viewer in the imagination.

But see the world from its Origin, and it's a different world. When we look at the world consciously from its Origin, it's a saved world, and in a certain sense it's a world that is OK, or more than OK—perfect. Heaven is Earth honestly perceived, truly perceived from the Perceiver, not from an imaginary station but from a real one.

How do you find your way to Heaven? How do you find your way Home? You have to know what the compass bearing is. Well, I can find that easily. It's not in that direction out into the world. It's in exactly the opposite direction, right to Here. It has a very specific compass bearing. It's right Here, and it's the land of the absolutely perfect and problem free. The thing is to get Here—and it's not too difficult because you never left.

Well, it follows that one's life in the light of this is post-resurrection. It is the new life. It is the post-mortem life, the risen life, the heavenly life. You say, "Well, let's explore this. In what respects is Heaven different from Earth? I shan't really take this seriously unless you show me a spectacular difference between the old experience and the new experience separated by death." Death makes the difference. You cross the river of death, and you come to a new world. It's got to be different before it will convince you that this is Heaven whereas the other one was not. And so we go into a whole list of things that are so utterly different: eating, walking, dying, sleeping. You name it, it's different.

Question: When I die, do I stop existing?
DEH: Here where you are, at least where I am Here, is this which cannot die because there is nothing to die.

But you say, "What happens after Douglas dies? Isn't this simple, sheer annihilation?" We have to look at the question of time. Afterlife, which goes on and on, with or without benefit of Douglas, what does that mean? I don't understand what life beyond the veil for Douglas means. Which Douglas goes to the other side? Is it young Douglas, middle-aged Douglas, or this old man? Or is it Douglas on his deathbed? And what does he do once he gets to the other side? Does he get older again? I don't understand all this business of what happens to the little guy when he goes beyond the veil. It's complete nonsense as far as I'm concerned.

But I am this One Here. Now this One is not in time; time is in it. The only life beyond death that I can perceive as possible—not only possible but laid on and obvious for me—is life which is not in time, which is eternal life, and it is life which is now and only now. From it time comes; into it time disappears. In this room now it is ten-to-ten. Right Here there is no time. When I bring the watch up to Here, it disappears. I'm supposed to be eighty-two years old. That little guy in the mirror certainly looks it. But when I look Here, I find I am exactly the same as I was when I was eight. I can't find any passage of time or any change at all. It is absolutely timeless Here. From it comes that little Douglas who is aging every minute and the world which is aging and perishing every minute. Here I find no change. I find Here the timeless origin of time.

This is another one of those metaphysical questions which just give us problems. I know it's a hard one to identify with the timeless one Here. We need to keep coming back, looking for the answers to simple questions like: How many eyes am I looking out of now? Is it one great Window or two little peepholes in a meatball? Are we face to face? Where do I stop? Stick to things like that, keep coming back to Who you are, grow in your trust of it, and these questions about eternity and time, these great metaphysical questions, will be answered not in intellectual terms but in real terms, and they won't matter anymore. They will answer themselves. But here we can't go further than that.

Question: *I met a woman this summer who believed in the Leonard Orr school of thought that you can physically live forever. I showed her your book, and she totally freaked out.*
DEH: That is crazy—to think that you needn't die, that you only die when you decide to die! And that if you want to live, you can live as this person, as Douglas, forever! That man is dotty!

We have the idea that survival of the individual is desirable.

First of all, I can't imagine a more horrible fate than to be Douglas forever and ever and ever. That would be absolute roaring hell—Douglas getting older and older and older, unable to be let off being Douglas. Absolutely unthinkable hell. In Greek mythology, the gods gave Tithonius that gift, and of course it was a disaster; he couldn't die. For me, the idea of going on forever, month by month, year by year is frightening. People do normally expect to do that and to meet their dear ones in heaven. But it hasn't really been thought through. The real eternal life is the timeless eternal life available now. Which of them is real, which does one want, which one does one live for? The eternal life now is totally available.

The other thing that makes what this chap is saying so dotty— that I can live as long as I like—is that he's saying I will outlast the Earth. The Earth is going to pack up and become a dead planet. I will outlast the Solar System? I will outlast this galaxy? As Leonard, how is he going to survive all those things? Floating in space? It's mad, isn't it? The Timeless is the answer to that one.

Question: Do you have any expectation regarding death? How do you relate to the evidence of psychic research?
DEH: There are two points here. One is that the mind, the psyche, this body of feeling and thought and so on, which is peripheral to Who I am, doesn't necessarily vanish at death. The evidence is overwhelming that it may hang around in time. It sometimes hangs around in unpleasant ways. When there's been a murder or some unresolved crisis, this thing becomes a sort of ghost or presence, and this is not to be desired. I don't want to haunt Nacton, thank you very much. In any case, it's rather brief, and I would say, at the end of Douglas's shelf life, enough is enough. Let me off being that one.

On the other hand, Who I really am has no future and no past. One is eternal now. One is not in time at all. This is the Timeless. This is what one is.

However, it is the nature of the Timeless to manifest in time, and I suppose the idea of reincarnation has a certain amount of truth in it—that the One Who I really am is forever incarnating and will continue to do so. But that's all I can say. I'll report further when more evidence comes in!

I think of death very frequently. One has to die daily. The skillful thing is that you put in a lot of homework before you actually find yourself on your deathbed. You'll need it then.

Question: What is mortification? Does it feature in this way or path?
DEH: Literally, mortification means dealing death out. To mortify something is to kill it. It is only when I am in despair of Douglas, really in despair of Douglas, totally persuaded of his incompetence, and, indeed, of all the nonsenses he gets up to—which is a kind of mortification—that I come back to the One I really am. If I try and put about fifty percent of my trust in Douglas and fifty percent of my trust on Who I really, really am, I'm going to make the worst of both worlds.

The arrow of inward attention is mortifying. When you do the onion-peeling experiment, very specifically you come to the regions of the human, the cellular, the molecular, the atomic, the subatomic, and then eventually nothing whatever. What is that but mortification, literally? It is mortification of all those identifications. It's the price of life, isn't it? It's the old, old story: die to live. Give your life. The way to have your life is to give it up, dying into the new life. The death of the little guy and the birth of the Big One.

My business in life is to get used to being Who I really, really am instead of just being little old Douglas. I've got to put in my practice now. Plato said that philosophy is the practice of death. That sounds miserable, but in fact it isn't. I've got to practice being Who I am now, in my heart giving up being Douglas. We live truly from this place where death dies.

This fact seems to me marvelous: the death that I die now is far more real than the death that is coming up, the official one. It's far more real in the sense that it is deliberate, it's repeated, it's conscious, it goes to the deepest depths, visibly, of my nature. It's not held up at the cellular level or the molecular level. It's not an unconscious slipping back into a dreamy shade. This is for real.

Of course, by mortification, some people mean I've got to chastise myself. There's sufficient chastisement in life itself. I'm not going to wear a hair shirt. Life is sufficiently hairy.

Question: Does deterioration in mental capacity stop you from seeing Who you are?
DEH: It's my experience that senility, which I find creeping up, doesn't stop my seeing Who I am. I shall never go senile, but my world will. The universe, considered from the First-Person point of view, begins for the infant as pretty chaotic and disorganized. I won't say it's a senile universe, but certainly it's an infantile universe, not organized. As I grow up, the universe, my universe, becomes more organized. In mid-life, at thirty-five, it's as organized as it will be. After thirty-five, forty-five, fifty-five, eighty-two, it's getting disorganized. I forget people's names. Senility creeps in. But it's my universe that is growing senile. Here I am Space again for a somewhat disorganized universe.

Question: Why do people sometimes seem afraid to look at Who they are?
DEH: There is a profound and well-based reason for this fear,

and the profound and well-based reason for this fear is surely that we have one basic fear, the fear of death and annihilation. Coming back Here, looking in at the Void, is an arrow, isn't it? We say the experiments are vehicles, but they're also arrows or bullets. They come and they kill you. It really is the end of you. The fear of death, the fear of annihilation—that's the real terror. The resistance to it is well-based. The *Diamond Sutra* says as much. Seeing into your void nature is naturally quite terrifying.

Of course, we have this fear that when we look in we'll find death and annihilation. But it is death and resurrection. We forget that this death of the little one, who is dying anyway, is accompanied by our resurrection as the whole scene. So instead of this in-seeing being death, it becomes the answer to the problem of death.

Face to No-Face

CHAPTER FIVE
The Mystery
of
Self-Origination

Question: On the map you have I Am Spirit *and* I Am Not, *and you often describe the* I Am Spirit *as arising mysteriously out of the* I Am Not. *Can you explain what you mean by this?*

DEH: Out there in the mirror I see Douglas, a human being, albeit intangible, albeit staring straight ahead in the opposite direction to me, and thin. In that region, I am human. I spread my arms, and I find that they embrace not only him but the whole 160-degree world. In that region, I am All. This side of the mirror, down here, I find my legs. Closer, I find my chest. Even closer, I find the bottom line where my chest fades off the field of vision. Right Here where I am pointing, I find not a face but aware Capacity, the bright *I Am* aware of itself as *I Am*. These two words, *I Am*, are the nearest I can find to express what I find Here. They are too complicated, but the best I can do verbally is to say, "I Am Here." How is this *I Am* arising? It arises mysteriously out of what I see Here, which is absolutely nothing. Looking Here, as it were behind the *I Am*, I find total mystery, not a trace of a trace even of *I Amness.*

Here the *I Am* is bright and clear. And here the *I Am Not* goes back into the Abyss of Mystery. How the *I am* arises out of nothing for no reason and with no help is just so staggering. For me, this is the great joy. I do think that God, if I may use the term, is absolutely bowled over by the mystery of his own self-invention or self-creation. And one is in on that act of absolutely nothing becoming awake to itself and being awake to itself, with the help of the universe it comes up with. Without the universe, I don't see much chance of the *I am* becoming awake.

Question: How do you get from Being to Non-Being? There seems to be a reflex in my mind. I've seen a thought, and then I want to see something that's before the thought or where the thought issues from. I seem to be stuck in the habit of looking for Non-Being to appear.
DEH: The extraordinary thing is that when I look out at things in the world, I am not seeing in its full sense. Because what I see is so complicated, I can never quite take it in, I forget it, I have to

scan it, and this takes time. It is a species of ignorance or blindness or smog in that direction. But when I look at Who I am, I find no smog. This view goes on and on forever into the Abyss of Mystery, the Abyss of Non-Being from which Being arises.

In this sense, the Mystery is the most accessible part of our lives. Was it Aristotle who said that nothing is so clear as Non-Being? We just have to drop words and look. Your problem might be that there are a few words and phrases hanging round there. Just look Here and take what you get. This is where your Center is. We look in this direction for our Resource. It's unknowable, unthinkable, utterly mysterious, but totally accessible. And it's where we're living from anyway, isn't it?

Question: I often feel that Consciousness is necessary for me to know my Non-Being, and that Non-Being depends on Consciousness.
DEH: I wouldn't differ from that. Nirvana doesn't exist without Samsara. Hui Hai puts it very poetically: "*Prajna* is unconscious, but facing the yellow flowers, it functions." This Non-Being is below Being, below Consciousness, below everything, so there's nothing Here to reveal, nothing Here to come up with. It's beyond and below everything. So how do you know anything about it? Well, you can see what it comes up with: the yellow flowers, the universe. And without the universe, as the expression of this ineffable Origin, there's no ineffable Origin.

I am sure that God, bless her heart, is thrilled by the universe, but I think her chief joy, her chief surprise and wonder, is wonder at her own self-origination for no reason and with no help—the mystery of Nothingness, unaware of itself, achieving Awareness, Non-Being flipping over into Being. And she doesn't know how she does it! She couldn't know how she does it! When we enjoy this, it is worship. It's not Douglas's worship of God. It's God's own astonishment at its, his, her invention, going on right Here, right Now. I wish I could put it more clearly. I just fail to put it into adequate words.

Question: You say that Consciousness arises from Nothing, but actually Consciousness itself is something, isn't it?
DEH: No. Consciousness is not something. Consciousness is *of* something. Consciousness has no parallel. We can't say what Consciousness is, not because we don't know it but because it is the only thing we do know—because we are it and it is indescribable. It is like nothing else. Gerard Manley Hopkins, the poet, says in an essay that between any two things in the world, I don't care how different they are, you will always find some connection. But between Consciousness and other things, there's no connection. It is in a class by itself. That is the mystery, and it is Who you are.

Question: Can you say more about the I Am Not?
DEH: The Sufis are insistent on this Nothingness, this absolute, absolute Nothingness, of which nothing can be said. It's the dark Abyss of Nothingness, totally without any being, life, or consciousness, a primordial foundation and base of the whole world. Now, it's enormously important to get a feel of that side of the picture; otherwise, one is saying something that I find particularly deadening, if not stupid—that there *has* to be Consciousness. There doesn't *have* to be anything at all. The natural state would be nothing whatever.

Question: When I see no face where I thought I had a face, I see nothing at all. Is this the No-thing you are talking about?
DEH: Yes, but it is No-thing awake to itself as No-thing. That's very special. The awakeness of the No-thing is the marvel, isn't it? It's not unaware. It's as though it's aware at the top and not

the bottom. It's the bottomless Abyss, the bottomless Well.

Why or how Consciousness should arise as it does from the blank inane Here, as it's doing all the time, is just incredible mystery. And if you call this God, I'm sure that God is absolutely astonished by his own impossible feat of self-origination. He doesn't know how he does it. If he knew how he did it, he would be missing out on the greatest joy imaginable, which is the wonder of Consciousness arising from Unconsciousness for no reason and with no help.

Human beings are so incredibly blasé. You show them something like this, and they say, "So what! What are you going on about? Of course Being has to be. Consciousness has to exist. Isness is natural." I think that God's hair stands on end in wonder at her own self-invention. It's impossible! It's that wonderful. Gosh, let me live from this realization, this astonishment.

Put it like this: we congratulate ourselves on various things, don't we? I congratulate myself on being English, perhaps. Ha ha! Why, I don't know. I congratulate myself on being male, which is even more ridiculous. I congratulate myself on not having Alzheimer's too badly at this time. A million things we congratulate ourselves on, give ourselves good marks for. But there's one thing that's superb, and we never realize what an incredible thing it is: *I Am*. I've occurred. Not I am this, not I am that, but just *I Am*. That is the great marvel. *I Am*! After that, a billion universes are chickenfeed.

This is so important for me because it puts in perspective my troubles. A Reality that can get off its own launching pad with no help and for no reason and invent itself and get cracking and produce the kind of universe we have—I trust the One who can do that. I'm not going to get too bogged down in the silly, quirky little details of Douglas's nonsenses. I'm not going to take my little self and my troubles so seriously, now I'm awake to this astounding miracle going on Here all the time. This mystery of what's behind the *I Am* puts the *I Am* and all the other stuff into perspective, and my problems become peanuts in the light of this amazing realization.

The trouble with our obsession with our human condition is that it is so boring and trivial. We encourage it to play up like a naughty child and give us a run for our money. Nisargadatta says that we have just to refuse to play that game. We refuse to follow the mind's contortions. They are like a naughty child who wants to draw attention to itself and draw attention from the wonder and splendor of Who we really are.

But this is all perhaps a rather personal thing. I do like to get it off my chest. It doesn't mean all that much to all my friends, I admit, but for some it does mean a very great deal.

Question: Calling It the Self-originating One is another way of naming the Unnamable, isn't it?
DEH: Well, it's not for me only a definition. Here's something I'm absolutely in awe of, something that fills me with wonder. The mystery and the wonder are absolutely crucial. The experience of self-origination isn't just intellectual. It is worship: abasement before the extraordinary fact that Existence exists for no reason and with no help. The One who is aware, who is more me than Douglas is me, who is aware *Here*, who is the universal Awareness in the world, this One is in awe—on present evidence—this One is in awe of its own self-origination with no help and for no reason.

The endless delight is the realization that one doesn't go round the world looking for this Abyss of Mystery in some place, somewhere else, in some abstract idea. It is present, it is now, it is concrete. It is right where I'm pointing. Right Here, when I point at what I suppose to be my face, I am pointing into the Abyss, the Mystery from which it all comes. I'm pointing at the Gulf from which Being emerges, the Factory that manufactures itself. Not a bit of it, not a part of it, not a sample of it, but the actual Gulf, which is now mysteriously producing these words about Itself. This is not Douglas reflecting on Being. It is Being raising its eyebrows at Itself, being bowled over by Itself.

Question: It's like a veil.
DEH: But that veil, being impenetrable, is where I can take my stand. When you can find something behind a veil, that's a different matter. But this is all veil, solid veil. To go forward in life not knowing who you are or where you're coming from is poetry. These people who use expressions like "the dark desert of the Godhead where God is unknown to Himself" speak to my heart very much. One casts oneself into that wild sea. What I can understand, what I can know, what I can get taped, will not satisfy my heart or my mind.

The thrilling bottom line is that I (I don't mean Douglas, I mean the real I) is absolutely hidden from itself. I know myself as unknowable. I'm rooted and grounded in complete mystery, unknowability, ineffability, unawareness.

Question: Is there a distinction between "nothing" and the "No-thing"?
DEH: Yes. A nothing that's awake to itself as nothing, to put it rather perversely, is quite something! Nisargadatta is clear about this, and one of the good things he says is that *I Am* is not the end of the story. Beyond the *I Am* is where the *I Am* comes from. The great Sufis are also clear on this, going behind Consciousness to the amazing awakening of Consciousness out of the dark night of Chaos, the dark night of Non-Being. Out of unimaginable nothingness, from that unconscious dark night, emerges for no reason the No-thing which is the light of Consciousness. And

it's happening now, and it's happening where you are, and you haven't a clue how or why—at least if you have, do tell me.

Eckhart makes the distinction between God and the Godhead. He says, "You can have God. I want the Godhead." The Godhead is beyond anything. You can't say anything about the Godhead. God is the *I Am*. He's got off the ground; he's got off his launching pad. But behind the *I Am* is the Ground, which is utter mystery. This is where our ultimate comfort lies, in the Mystery.

Let me put it like this: by rights there should be nothing whatever. It's incredibly unnatural that Consciousness is. This is the most wildly improbable, impossible thing. It's impossible, and it is! After this achievement, has anything gone wrong? Can anything go wrong? Isn't this the ultimate guarantee of the goodness, the rightness, the incredible value at the heart of everything? This Perfection, the Perfection which achieves the impossible every moment, namely itself, is an incredible underwriting of the value of the world, the value of our life. It invents itself. I call that clever!

Question: So this sense of the impossibility is more than a way of speaking.
DEH: Yes. It makes all the difference. I can be aware of the Aware Emptiness, its function as the place where the fullness comes from, with an implicit feeling that it's just got to be, that it's reasonable; it doesn't take my breath away and knock me out. It just is. It's just as given as that table is given. There it is. But the other way of looking at the matter doesn't take any of that for granted. It says that by rights nothing should exist. It's most irregular. It's breaking all the rules. And it's you who are doing it right Here. It's not a miracle that is happening somewhere else. It's taking place right Here, right Here. You are a magician bring-

ing yourself out of this hat of Non-Being, and you haven't a clue how you are doing it. I take my stand on that which I cannot understand.

It's got a quality which is like nothing else on Earth for me. There's nothing to match it, a quality which is absolutely unique and quite inexplicable. Look, there is only one Awareness—multiple Consciousnesses I find no evidence for—call it God or the *I Am* or your True Self. Call it what you wish. And this one Awareness lives in constant wonderment at its achievement of Awareness, totally in the dark about how it's done, and rejoicing in that darkness like mad. I'm impossible, it says to itself, and yet here I am. Bang, here I am.

Question: Have you always felt this?
DEH: The feeling goes back into the mists of my very early childhood. I can't tell you exactly. I can't even speculate accurately about how it arose, but it's very natural for children to ask these questions and to rejoice in them and to be bowled over by them. The formula is very simple. The child asks his mum who made the world, knowing very well what she'll say. She answers, "God." He does a little think and says, "OK. God made the world, but who made God?" His mother is sensible. She doesn't say, "Don't ask silly questions." She says, "Well, he made himself." "You mean," says the child, "there was absolutely nothing, nothing, nothing, and zchuk! up he popped, with a long white beard? He made himself? This is impossible. Out of nothing, nothing, nothing, zchuk! up he came with his beard streaming in the wind? How did he do it?" "I don't know," says the mother. Perhaps she even says that people are not supposed to know. The child is fobbed off with answers like that, and he finally gets the message that these kinds of questions are stupid or not the questions to ask. God is a fait accompli. Then all the heart and worship and

wonder at his true nature and origin is rubbed out in this stupid adult common sense, which is actually nonsense.

Question: I have always wondered about my own birth, and I realize now that what you are talking about is exactly the same birth that I went through. There was nothing, and all of a sudden the universe was there.
DEH: Yes. God was in at her own birth, a virgin birth. God was really, really startled at her own achievement. She bore herself. That's quite something, to be her own mother and father.

Question: That's exactly what we each do.
DEH: That's right. We recapitulate that. As Who we really are, we go through this process of the birth of God. Our true birth is the birth of God—not the birth that was registered in a book and became official with a birth certificate.

Question: How important for you is sharing this sense of wonder?
DEH: The strange thing is that one meets very few people to whom this is immediately exciting, apparent, wonderful, but one does occasionally meet such friends. I can think of three or four for whom it is all-important. I try to share this with all my friends ultimately, and quite a lot of my dearest and longtime friends say, "Douglas, I don't quite get what you are talking about." And others do get what I'm saying. I'm not separating them into deep people and shallow people, but some get excited about it, some don't quite get it, and some say, "Well, yes, it is rather strange."

I have a friend who couldn't make out at first what I was talking about. At least he thought I was getting excited about nothing much, or he thought it was a rather "Douglasy" adventure that he didn't particularly share. Why go on and on about the impossibility or improbability of Being and Awareness? After a few months, though, he came to me and said, "I get it. It's absolutely staggering." I do think the feeling needs to be roused. It's a good thing to talk about and get around, perhaps not only amongst one's immediate friends. It's something to noise abroad because there are people there waiting for this joy. It's as though the tinder needs a spark to light it up.

We can encourage each other. It's something we can do for the world, and we needn't be shy: this is so deep and so fundamental that we may be sure that in talking about it we are appealing to the profoundest of all levels in people, to their deepest hearts. They would and will have every reason to be grateful because this is so precious. If you've got this, you've got what for me is the most precious thing of all.

Paradoxically, very strangely, this for me is the crème de la crème, the highest of the high, the most precious of all things spiritual, and yet in a certain sense, this dimension of total mystery is not the final stage. And for this reason: it is a thought, and it is a feeling. It's something that comes and goes. You see, it happens now at three o'clock. You can say, "Well, I had it good and strong on Thursday, but on Friday it wasn't around." It's infinitely the most precious feeling and thought one could possibly have, but still it's a thought and a feeling.

Now, the final thing Here is neither a thought nor a feeling, and it neither comes nor goes. Seeing Who You Are puts its money on absolute Clarity, Emptiness, No-Thingness, and that is unchanging, invulnerable. That is the Abyss itself. The first fruit of the Abyss is the wonder, but the Abyss is deeper even than the wonder, and seeing Who you are plunges you in that Abyss. So if you have a friend who says, "I don't know what you are talking about, this Mystery," you say, "Fine, chum." God, it's an incredible extra, but it is an optional extra. For me it is so precious, but it does come, and it does go. Perhaps one spends a week without ever thinking of it, and that's all right, that's proper.

Question: If you are judging whether you are truly seeing Who you are by whether you are appreciating the Mystery, you might be setting yourself up for anxiety.

DEH: Of course. You say, "Oh, I haven't been enjoying this for a long time. I can't be seeing clearly," or "I'm slipping." Nonsense. It becomes an idol immediately. So it's a bonus, a pleasure, a sauce to the real meal. It's an aperitif, not the meal itself. The real nourishment is the bare, bare sight of one's Nature. That's the real nourishment, isn't it? And the rest is, after all, I suppose, partly a matter of different gifts. We have different gifts, and we have different insights. We are a varied lot, thank God. We are not built to some standard pattern.

Go for the plain, go for what some mystics call the dryness, go for the desert, go for what is totally featureless, and you will get everything else. Go for even the most glorious and wonderful of those products, those fruits, those features, the oasis in the desert, go for any of that, and you've lost the heart of the matter.

Question: The Void or the Desert is not actually separate from the world, is it? You can't find it without looking both ways.

DEH: That's right. If you go for the Origin, you get the world. If you go for the world without the Origin, you don't even get the world. You get bits and pieces of it, a fragmented world. The only thing that holds the world together is where you are coming from at this moment. It saves the world.

Question: When you talk about the Mystery being a resource, what do you mean?

DEH: Seeing Who you are is one thing. You may say trusting is another. And rejoicing in the wonder is a third. How are they all connected? Well, they are very deeply connected, of course. The ultimate resource, which is quite basic and always available, underlying everything, is the bare seeing. But in my experience, I have to go on seeing very earnestly and very faithfully for a long time and to test it out, to live it, to be it, to use it in the world before the trust in it grows. The trust is a dimension which is so important. If there is spiritual growth at all, it is growth in trusting This—and trusting This above all things. Put your trust in nothing but This, and then everything can be used.

Why should I put my trust in it? Why should it be so trustworthy, so reliable? One of the reasons is its incredible achievement of Being. That makes it trustworthy, even more than the fruits one perceives from time to time in peace and joy coming from this. If I can't trust this Awareness, which can be trusted to somehow emerge out of the dark night of obliteration, nothingness, what can I trust? It's an incredible trick. Staggering. We are certainly free to use anything the world offers—psychotherapies, devices, and assistance of every possible kind—but on what do we put our money? Do we put our shirts on those means, or do we put our shirts on what is trustworthy, this Mystery, this Origin?

The wonder is valuable for me in that it promotes trust. To trust is to hand over to, isn't it? Well, I hand over to the Mystery, and it's trustworthy. It never fails. It's as the *Tao Te Ching* says, a bottomless well, never running dry. The Mystery and the trustworthiness go together.

Question: Does it connect to the feeling that nothing can go wrong?
DEH: Yes—well, the feeling that ultimately, nothing has gone wrong. This is the trust I'm talking about.

Question: Does it work for specific situations in your life?

DEH: It certainly is not trust that everything will go according to the way Douglas would like and would love for his friends—that all is going to be well in human terms, that tragedy is going to be avoided, or that there won't be the usual problems and troubles attendant on human life. I don't see these being mitigated. I don't see them being reduced. I see them carrying on as usual. It seems extraordinary to say it, but one has a feeling that, viewed from their origin—which, in fact, is the only place they can be viewed from—things are all right. They are all right.

One thinks of the horrors of the world, the cruelty, the things one can see absolutely no good in at all. One thinks of the concentration camps of Hitler, one thinks of cruelty to children and animals, one thinks of the people who from the start have ghastly handicaps and trouble of every kind, mental and physical—one thinks of all this, and one's heart bleeds for such people. Or one thinks of people who at the end are just rubbed out by society because they are so wicked. Think of someone like the Yorkshire Ripper going to prison. I am he. He didn't choose to be the Yorkshire Ripper. The agony of that man when he reflects on what he means to his fellows. How can that be all right? It can be all right by my being him. I can save the situation—not Douglas but Who I really am can somehow get behind and be him. And this is what is meant by God's love saving the world.

It's a mystery, and I don't understand it, but I'm absolutely sure that, looked at this way, everything is ultimately all right. But it's all right because from this Origin one then goes out and is all things, and the world is saved somehow and the world is all right from the Mystery. It is itself a mystery. I can't exactly explain why it seems absolutely, absolutely all right. Dostoevsky has in a number of places this sense of the all-rightness of these horrors. I don't understand it, but I am quite sure of it.

Chapter Five

Question: Have you found the realization of the mystery of Being expressed in religious or philosophical writings?
DEH: I've searched the scriptures for some very clear indication of this realization, and I think it is growing. It's something that's come later rather than earlier in the history of spiritual thought. I've read all I can find in translation of the Hindu scriptures, the *Upanishads*, mainly, and I've never found the term *Self-originating One* or *the mystery of Self-origination*. I don't find a direct reference to it even in such a great man as Chuang Tzu, third century B.C. I don't find any reference in the Bible to God's sense of his own impossibility or improbability. There, God is taken as a fait accompli.

Some of the Gnostics, who were almost eliminated in the early Christian world, got hold of this, and they used the term *the Self-originating One*. God is described as being a mystery to himself. He is bowled over by himself because of his self-origination. God worships himself as unknowable. True worship is the sense that impossibility is being achieved without any knowledge of how it is done. I find it in the medieval book, *The Book of Privy Counsel*, which is contemporary with *The Cloud of Unknowing*. It sounds like a guide to lavatories, doesn't it? In *The Book of Privy Counsel*, there's a marvelous idea: it's not so much *what* God is but *that* God is which is adorable. The fact of God! Being self-originating! Then Angelus Silesius in the Seventeenth Century: "God bends and bows, and to himself doth pray." God bends and bows to himself because he *is*, for no reason. You have a partial recognition of this in Ludwig Wittgenstein, the near-contemporary philosopher. He said it is not *what* the world is but *that* it is which is mystical. It's the wonder and awe. I don't think Wittgenstein goes nearly far enough because he's talking about the world, the universe. Well, the universe is not mystical. It's not that the universe is but that Consciousness is, that God is, that Awareness is, which is mystical. Awareness invents itself. Without reason, without help. Pop!

This realization seems to be around now, and it is very encouraging. We are apt to think of these times as the latter days when we are falling away from the golden age of mystical experience. We are hoodwinked by the scriptures. We think that the wise men of old knew everything, that it must be there in the scriptures. The boot is on the other foot. It's given to us in modern times to have new insights of the most precious kind into Who we are. We are living in a most incredible, creative, beautiful, wonderful, dangerous, but marvelous time when new revelations, new techniques are coming up strongly. Although one has enormous respect for the scriptures, gosh, they don't cover the whole country. Who we really, really are does. What is so marvelous about the *I Am* is that it is self-originating. The mystery of self-origination! Consciousness! There doesn't have to be Consciousness. I find it most extraordinary. And I think God, Who we really, really, really are, is absolutely bowled over. Pulling yourself up out of nothingness by your own nonexistent bootstraps is a very impressive performance.

Of course, the performance itself is timeless. We have been talking as if it goes on through time, as if this fountain of Awareness arising out of unawareness is primarily a thing which is serial and goes on and on. That's what it appears to be at the top end of it where time emerges. But it's absurd to regard time as proceeding from time. Time comes from the timeless Abyss. That's another part of the Mystery. So when one talks about this realization emerging rather late in the history of spiritual understanding and mystical experience, one is talking about the top end of it, so to say. Time needs change. Change needs something to change. And if it's empty of everything, time cannot be there. Self-origination is timeless.

Chapter Five

Question: There's a story about Shiva sitting in deep meditation before the world has been created. Suddenly a beautiful dancing creature appears before him. He did it, but he didn't know how he did it. "My God," he said, "what have I done?"

DEH: Yes, but this presupposes Shiva. I'm going back of Shiva. I buy Shiva being present and creating the world. That's obvious. Obviously, existing, he can go on with the business of more existence. But what about his own existence? I don't find that question asked in the story.

On the other hand, increasingly I've been feeling not only the primary mystery of the Origin but also the secondary mystery of the world. I do things like talk or move my hand. How do I know the end of this sentence before I start it? And then how do the orders go through in time to these little chaps—my cells— to push and pull at the requisite moment so that I can move my hand? Think of the miracle of organization here. It would baffle a top business house to run the business of moving one's little finger so smoothly and so swiftly. And this miracle is multiplied billions of times all over the universe. Think of all the atoms going round so busily and properly. God, it is a fabulous machine. And nobody's standing over it with a stopwatch, you know, sacking employees for doing it wrong. What keeps the darn thing going?

The ordinary man thinks that God knows all about the world, and that scientists know a lot about the world that he doesn't. Well, neither God nor the scientists know a lot about the world, to be truthful. Especially God, who doesn't know it at all. Insofar as my information goes, the one who is bowled over about the world is God. The myth is that science is on the edge of getting it all taped. A real scientist doesn't think anything of the kind. It's the popular idea. And the religious idea, the religious myth is that God is running it all very carefully, cleverly supervising the behavior of every dust-grain. This wouldn't make him into a God at all, but into a Monstrous Apparatchick. Think of all the silly things he would have to look after, like the behavior of every sand grain in the Sahara Desert. No, God has no idea how it all works. He is consumed with wonder at his own unbelievable success. I think God just sits back and his hair stands on end with the wonder. He doesn't try to run it. These things are so mysterious they deserve another name than *mystery*. They're more mysterious than mysterious.

Where does one take one's stand, after all we've said and enjoyed together? I can only say I take my stand on what I sometimes call the Idiocy Here. I look Here, and I go blank; I have no idea. Here is a region of no ideas, of no will, of no realization, of no enlightenment, of absolute freedom from all that. And the will and the enlightenment and the enjoyment and the mystery, all this is centrifugal, going outwards from Here. Looking Here, the Origin is clear of it all. Here's the only safe place to take one's stand. Here's where one is anyway, where one is free of all that stuff. What we've been doing is gathering a little harvest of fruits there. They are very precious and valuable and sweet fruits. But the root is not like that.

Question: It's very paradoxical. I suppose it depends on the time and place, but you go to the place where there isn't any mystery, where there isn't any will, and mystery and will pop up. But look for mystery and will, and . . .

DEH: And they vanish. I know. You attend to the source, and let everything else come. It's so simple. You water the root of the plant. You don't water the leaves and the branches. You water the root. And the root is darkness. It's so wonderful. It's so wonderful. Gosh. What an astonishment this all is. Just think of how one takes things for granted. Fait accompli. We take things for granted. It's so wonderful. Unbelievable. Rich. And terrible.

Question: What do you mean, terrible?
DEH: Well, one can't deny the tragic and terrible side of it. That's where the Indian conception of Kali, the Black Goddess, one hand creating the universe and the other destroying it, is so relevant. That's an aspect of the whole thing, isn't it? The tragedy of the world, and the pain and the ghastliness of the world, are things we can't afford to gloss over and be all cheerful about. One of the things that connects up with our sense of mystery is a growing feeling for the suffering of the world. Strangely, the answer to the problem of pain is to not forget about the agony of so many, to take it on board. If we go for the mystery and all these lovely spiritual delights just by themselves, we can be led astray.

Again, these feelings come naturally. They are not for cultivating. The natural history of seeing Who we are, if it's working at all, does result in an increasingly tender heart. Sometimes I feel the dry-as-dust talk of the Void and of everything being taken care of in the Nothingness means something has gone wrong. It's not been allowed to grow in the natural way it would grow into involvement with the world. One is the world, and one can't separate oneself from any of the suffering. One is out there being the world. One isn't sitting in a nice, comfortable, detached place contemplating voidness.

Face to No-Face

CHAPTER SIX
Surrender

DEH: All this seeing business is a wonderful gate, but for me, what the gate opens on, the meaning of the story, the heart of the matter, in a certain sense, is not the seeing; it is the surrender.

Question: What are you surrendering to?
DEH: Well, I'm talking about the will. It seems to me there are three levels of will. The ordinary, common-or-garden sense of will is what Douglas wants, which is to go and have a meal presently, say. The next level is the psychological unconscious, which may have a totally different intention, perhaps to go and be sick or not to want a meal. Sometimes the second level is the exact opposite of the first, especially in Jungian psychology. These two

levels belong to the little one. But there's a third level, which is not the little one at all but is the Big One. And what is the will of the Big One? The will of the Big One is that everything shall be as it is. If you like to talk in terms of God, the will of the Big One is God's will. When I move from the superficial will of the little one, Douglas, to the will of the One I really am, then I find satisfaction.

Question: When you say: let everything be as it is, does that include the will of the little one?
DEH: Well, it's for acceptance, isn't it? We're talking very loosely. The little one doesn't actually have a will. But I can't stress enough that until the will is surrendered, there is no peace.

Question: Is it correct to say that surrender is not about surrendering to what is out there but to this Here, and then all else follows.
DEH: Yes. Every "choice" that is made from *not* knowing, from *not* having it all taped, from *not* having it in a briefcase, from *not* having a script or a rule, but from the Clarity Here and what fills it—seems to me to be a whole different deal, the true surrender. Then you surprise yourself. You say, "Gosh, did I say that? That was interesting. I never thought I was going to say that." There's good authority for this if you need authority. Jesus said, "When you're called up before the magistrate, don't think what you're going to say in advance. You'll be given the words at the moment." It applies to all choices, doesn't it? You see Who you are and find out what you do. Often you can't see the consequences. It may be that somebody needed you to say that or be like that. Something in the world had to be done. You don't know. See Who you are and find out what you get up to.

Question: Let's say I have a job that I don't like, but I surrender to it because this is the way things are. That doesn't seem very intelligent. How do we make choices when we understand surrender to be accepting the way things are?

DEH: Yes, but accepting things as they are, surrendering to what's given, would surely include surrendering to the fact that you've got a rotten old job and you want to change it. You surrender to that too, don't you?

Question: How do we reconcile choice with surrender?

DEH: We all have to choose. We have to choose whether to have All Bran or muesli for breakfast, to sit in this comfortable chair or an uncomfortable one. Our life is choice all the time. But the question is: Am I putting Here a very limited chooser called Douglas, or am I seeing Douglas off and living from Who I really, really, really am Here? Still the choices have to be made. The question is: Who is making them?

Question: When I have a decision to make, do I just simply sit back and wait?

DEH: With some you can afford to wait and with some you can't. The decision about whether I should get up and go to the loo I have to make rather quickly, don't I?

I suggest there are, or should be, three stages of what we are up to. The first stage is to see Who we are and really get that clear. The second stage is to go on seeing it until it is our lifestyle, until we do it naturally. But along with the first two stages and growing all the time comes number three. That is trust—trusting Who we really, really, really are. And that means that when I have to act, I'm not acting from the resources of that little one in the mirror but from the resources of the *I Am* this side of the mirror. There's no in-between. Either I am putting my money on that hopelessly inefficient, dying image—it's just a paper-thin picture on that pathetic object whose name is Douglas—or I am putting my money on where I am coming from, on the Mystery that has this incredible know-how and certificate of ability, that it *is*. Now, that is quite a certificate. And so I trust This. When I have to make a decision, which happens all the time, what I do is refer it back Here. In other words, I see Who I am, and then I see what I get up to. See Who you are, and trust Who you are to come up with the right answer at the right time.

Question: St. John of the Cross, De Caussade, and The Cloud of Unknowing *all say we should live in and trust that darkness of not knowing.*
DEH: That's right. It's all about not knowing, not understanding, leaning back on the Mystery. We have This for backing. We are backed by God.

Question: Does that mean trusting confusion?
DEH: I have a little bit of a job trusting confusion. I would trust the Uncomplex that complexity and confusion come from.

Question: You accept the confusion?
DEH: You *accept* the confusion, and you *trust* What the confusion comes from.

This is all about spontaneity and authentic living from Who you are, without preview, unselfconsciously. But this doesn't mean you don't prepare and you don't think about what to do. It's not just giving up on the problem and waiting till the answer pops up. I think it's often extremely appropriate to study the question, look at the pros and the cons, set it out in array, think about it, make tables about it, write down the options, study it as much as you like, and then put it in a drawer and sleep on it. Then when the decision has to be made, you'll find it is quite likely to be the right one coming up from Who you are.

Question: Is surrender the same as following your feelings in the moment?

DEH: It depends what you mean by feelings. My feelings are in fact very stereotyped and predictable and "Douglasy". They are terrifically conditioned. If I'm being led by my feelings, I react in typical ways. However, the clear perception of the Space Here is not a matter of feeling. This cool Capacity for feeling is upstream of feeling itself. So I'm not reacting. Dante says, "Blessedness comes from vision, not from feeling or loving, which comes later." First comes the Vision and the Clarity, not because feelings aren't enormously important but because they are downstream of Who we really, really are.

Question: Does surrender result in bliss?

DEH: I have difficulty with the word *bliss* because seeing Who I am is available when I would hardly describe my state as blissful. But I suppose that however unblissful my experience, however uncomfortable I am, when I come Home and am Space for the sadness and unblissfulness, there does seem to be a peace, a serenity, which is independent of the pain. Very strange. I don't know what to call it.

There is a difference between suffering that is resisted and suffering that is taken on board. It is in the acceptance of it that the peace comes. Eckhart says that you have to get to the absolute end of all your resources, and then the divine power suddenly breaks through. But we're so apt to stay a little bit short, aren't we, resisting to the last, fighting. For me it's a physical thing. It's as though you say when you're breathing out, with St. John of the Cross, I know nothing, I have nothing, I am nothing. Your shoulders and arms flop. I know this is a personal quirk, but for me, if a thing can take physical form, it's very much more effective. I think surrender is partly physical. It is something which happens to your body.

Question: You sometimes talk about an experience you call the Barrier, which sounds like the Dark Night of the Soul of St. John of the Cross. Can you explain what it means?
DEH: Well, it's not an easy question to answer. I guess it's different for different people, and one can't speak about other people with any confidence here. All I can say really is that in my own life I'm quite sure I've experienced something very like the Dark Night of the Soul. It could not have been more traumatic or more distressing.

Question: What happened?
DEH: Well, if you think of everything negative, that was about it. I'd been talking about Seeing Who you are for years, believing in it, thinking of it, sharing it, and I felt that I was still a mess, incredibly inadequate. I was shocked at myself for being so unregenerate, so short of what I was talking about. I felt that I had lost the love and confidence of my friends for good reason, that I wasn't somehow genuine, that my words far exceeded my performance. It wasn't that I ceased seeing Who I was because I couldn't do that, but it seemed that everything had gone wrong in an inexplicable way and that I was abandoned by God and man somehow. It was totally foolish because on every count I was persuaded that this was not so, and yet it occurred. It's a mystery.

These experiences are perhaps brought on by circumstances which are very painful. My interpretation is that the seeing part is just easy thing after easy thing. Though in a certain sense it is hard because we have to keep it up, it's an easy one in the sense that every act of seeing Who you are is as easy as winking. But the giving up of the personal will is a hard one. It really is a hard one. And until the problem of the will is addressed, I think we are immature spiritually. When that problem is overcome, we can go on to what Evelyn Underhill, in *Mysticism*, calls union. It is a highly individual thing. One cannot dictate for other people. But for me it was just despair of myself and above all of my spiritual life.

Question: *How long did it last?*
DEH: It's a bit difficult to remember. I would have thought that at its worst it wasn't longer than six weeks. But then it spread over beyond that. It's also possible to get previews and postscripts. It's not something that's absolutely on and off.

Question: *Was it like depression?*
DEH: Yes, it was probably a profound depression. It's a mystery. It's quite possible that some people don't have to go through it, in which case they are very fortunate. It was an accumulation of my mounting distrust of myself, and probably necessary before I could put my trust in what was not myself.

Question: *Were you seeing Who you were throughout the experience?*
DEH: Oh, yes, absolutely, no question about that. So it is a mystery, isn't it? At one time, I thought that it was culturally conditioned and that Christians got it because they anticipated it. I thought it was not common and not pronounced in Hinduism or Buddhism or Taoism. But now I suspect that there must be something similar to it in those faiths. It's a mystery. It is really all about surrender of the will.

Question: *Did you lose your trust in seeing?*

DEH: Yes. During that time, the trust went. It was really irrational. I was overtaken by fear. I was seeing quite clearly. I'd all the theory of it. In fact, I'd had the practice of it for many years. But I was still an abandoned soul, a lost soul. There was no hope. It was brief, but the trust went.

Question: And how did you come out of it?
DEH: I just gradually got better. I accepted it. I was not rebelling against it as an experience so much. The way through it, I'm sure, is the constantly renewed surrender of one's superficial personal will to one's deepest will, which is, after all, the Agony in the Garden. There's the paradigm, the model of it.

When people pass through the Dark Night of the Soul, something very radical has happened. They have touched bottom, and they need to. They have really been down into hell, and they know what it is about. It is something that happens to people who are very serious about the spiritual life, and for the most part have been following it for years. You would think that the spiritual life would be a more or less steady progress to union with God, without any disasters en route. But not so. This is a comparatively late stage in the spiritual life.

Question: It's like the story of Job, isn't it?
DEH: Yes, indeed. A wonderful story. And of course the end of the story of Job is exactly what the end of one's own story is. "I have heard of Thee with the hearing of the ear, and now mine eye seeth Thee, and I abhor myself and repent in dust and ashes." A very moving story, one of the earliest in the Bible, actually. Job says a marvelous thing: "Though He slay me, yet will I trust in Him." Marvelous. That's the kind of thing that brings one through.

Chapter Six

Question: Are there times when you see Who you are but it doesn't seem like a refuge to you?

DEH: Very much so. Seeing Who one is, the simple vision Here, is the root. In my experience, it is without quality. It has Nothing to recommend it. It's naked, absolutely naked, and that is why it is so valuable—why it is available whatever one's mood. One doesn't have to psych oneself up. The leaning back and the comfort and the excitement and the sense of mystery and wonder with which This is connected for me—all these, however rich and important, seem to me to be just a little downstream from the Seeing. And this is a good thing because the Seeing, the Clarity, unites us all even if and when we don't appreciate the comfort and mystery, and when all seems gray and dull.

Question: The comfort and the mystery come and go?
DEH: Yes.

Question: What do you mean, then, as you said earlier this morning, that It never, never lets you down?

DEH: I mean that when I consciously give up on Douglas and invoke the support of my Backing, when I lean back on that, give up in favor of that, things come out the way they should— not necessarily good or comforting for Douglas in the immediate term, but in the long term, what's needed.

Question: Is relying on Who you are connected to the mystery of self-origination?

DEH: It is. The Mystery—where we are coming from, what is behind us, the Awareness which is our true nature—has the supreme and utterly unimaginable know-how to get off its own launching pad and invent itself. If it is that inventive, that creative, that skillful, that reliable, it would be a good thing to try it on the tiny comings and goings of our problematic life.

Question: Do you have any special ways to remind yourself to trust?
DEH: Yes. We all have our special ways. I remember one year at the Buddhist Society Summer School, I had a little insurance policy. I'd got a card with some notes on how to do my evening lecture. When I got to the lecture hall, I took a risk and threw the card away. The chairman introduced me politely, and I duly stood on my hind legs and faced the company of a hundred and twenty very earnest and learned Buddhists. I stood there, and nothing happened. I really was stuck. I just wasn't prepared. It would have been skillful, I suppose, to have at least got the first sentence ready. But I hadn't. I stood there, feeling more and more embarrassed. There was a bit of squirming going on, both on the platform and in the audience. I thought, "Really, this is the most embarrassing thing. Here's this chap standing on his hind legs and nothing is coming out." However, patience was rewarded on both sides. Something eventually did emerge. Once it started, the flow was not copious but was sufficient to get by with.

Well, I had a friend in the audience, and she came to me afterwards and said, "Douglas, that was very good." I was staggered. I didn't mention this embarrassment, this terrible, ghastly beginning. I said, "What was good about it?" And she said, "Oh, the thing that impressed me was you standing there in silence before anything happened."

Of course, it's a silly story. But I do think perhaps it was a simple instance, an early one, of not being frightened to rely on the Unknown. It's perfectly appropriate to think again and again and again, and rehearse things, and have an idea of what you are going to do. If it's a very important occasion, the more preparation you do, the better. This is not ruled out. But on the way there or when you go up to the platform and get on your hind legs, you just forget it all and find out what happens. Nine times out of ten, it owes something to that preparation, but not very much, perhaps. And sometimes quite the opposite of what you had prepared comes out, though I think what you had prepared is not wasted.

This is an example regarding public speaking, but it applies to other things. I'll give you an instance. I've got an issue to take up with a friend. I've got some ideas about how to do it, but when I meet him, I've got to ditch those ideas and listen to what comes out. Also, when I don't know and give up, I get great surprises. There were three or four things that came up last night at the workshop that I had never thought of before, never said before. They came up because Douglas was not responsible.

An essential ingredient of this trusting is that you are not excited about any apparent success. You just cannot take any credit. It's done in spite of Douglas, not because of Douglas. It happens because Douglas is not functioning at the Center. To take credit for it is a temptation, and to be excited about it is to hinder and delay its repetition. Furthermore, when you've been taken over and have been surprised by what comes out, and what comes out is authentic and works because it's not a personal reaction, it is appropriate then not to forget this but—it sounds very Christian—say "Thank you!" Don't take it for granted. Say "Thank you. Thank you, Lord, you really looked after me then." I know it's Yourself you are thanking in the deepest sense, but it's also Other than yourself that you are thanking. Taking it for granted and not being grateful is to discourage this inspiration.

Question: Has this trusting grown with you over the years?
DEH: Oh, very much. Years ago, after a workshop like last night, I would feel a little bit chirpy. I won't say euphoric, but in a good mood. But in recent years, it doesn't make any difference, and it

is really rather sobering. I think excitement is always dubious stuff in this region. If you are excited about it, look out. Or rather, look in!

Question: On the other hand, the trust does feel liberating.
DEH: Why yes, indeed. And it makes sense too in a very practical way. Here's a situation. I'm going to speak to a hundred people. I don't know them. I sit in my study, and I make some notes and plan what I will say—in the absence of those people, in the absence of the atmosphere. It's all Douglas speculating about what he should say in the future. If I go into the situation not knowing what to do and open myself to what some people call the vibes, there's a chance that what I say will be what is needed at that time and could not have been foreseen. On the other hand, planning isn't wrong even for the littlest things, provided it's tentative and no fixture.

There's a wonderful chapter in De Caussade's *The Sacrament of the Present Moment*, in which he describes the spiritual life as very much like the life of *whim*. Of course, the necessary background of this life is that you have in your heart handed over from who you think you are to Who you really are. Then, he says, when for no reason you feel an urge to write a letter to someone or go to see someone or do something unusual, and you don't know why, trust that urge and act accordingly. Quakers also talk about this, the inner guidance of the Holy Spirit. Say you are at a loose end. You don't know quite what to do for an hour. You might just go up to the bookcase and run your eye along the shelf and pick a volume. I don't say that it is, or isn't, a magic way of finding a treasure. Just try it. Or you may want to do a bit of cooking or go for a walk or telephone somebody. Seeing Who you are, you trust these indications of what to do, and therefore time doesn't hang heavy. It's a life guided by inner inspiration without your figuring everything out or knowing why you are doing it. If it's done from an image of the little one Here, it's whimsy and it's showing off and it's being eccentric and silly and irresponsible. If it's done from the vision of Who you really, really are Here, then extraordinary things do happen.

Sometimes I get stuck in my work. I don't know what the next chapter is to be, or I've got something wrong with this chapter. Or when I've finished a book, I don't know what to do next or which of about four projects is the one to develop. There is an awkward period between jobs. It might be a month or two when I'm trying this and trying that, and I have to be prepared to give up project after project before it's clear what I should do. It's a rather testing period, the doldrums. De Caussade, again, is enormously good about this. He says we should be prepared to be like broken pots waiting for the inspiration that is necessary. Be prepared to wait. It answers.

Everything I do is either coming from my human nature, from my Douglas image illegitimately and nonsensically superimposed on the Center of my life, or else it is coming from what is at the Center of my life, from Who I am. The difference between those two kinds of action doesn't look like much, but it is very, very deep. You could sum up the authentic one as not knowing. Only don't know.

Question: Does seeing Who you are help with pain?
DEH: Look at your hand. It's form-of-your-hand there to no form where you are. It's color there to no color where you are. Now prod your finger with your thumbnail. The pain is there in your finger, isn't it? Just like the form and color, is there any pain where you are? It's pain there to no pain Here. Here is the region free of pain, absolutely free of pain. Pain is a part of the world, and

the world is a painful old place, but at the Center of the world is a painless region, and that's where you always are. The rule is asymmetry. Color to no color, form to Void, pain to ease or lack of pain. The pain is not the same when it is felt and seen in this way.

Question: *You say that it is pain to no pain, and yet ultimately there is no separation, is there?*

DEH: Right. Distance is an illusion, and you do become the pain. But also there is a freedom. God takes on the pain of the world, and paradoxically God is free of the pain of the world. In the realm of deep things, it's always paradox.

There is a mystery about pain. It's the most hated thing; pain is a ghastly thing. Pain is the trouble, really, that we all suffer from—pain mental, spiritual, physical. But it is a mystery. C.S. Lewis wrote a book called *The Problem of Pain*, and Christianity does address this problem in practice. Its story is that through pain, through the acceptance of pain, through taking it on, through not running away from it, you come to something which couldn't be got by any other route. You get the perversion of this in the self-flagellation of some medieval monks and nuns. There were orgies of self-inflicted pain. But it is not for nothing that pain and the deepest and most wonderful experiences of life are very deeply associated, and those experiences cannot be had at the cost of no pain. We don't want it to be like that, but it is like that. Take someone like St. Francis of Assisi or Father Pio with the stigmata. St. Francis of Assisi was so taken up with the pain of the crucified Christ, so devastated by that young man's suffering, that he developed the stigmata, the five wounds in his hands and feet and side. So was Father Pio in Italy quite recently. St. Francis, who had such excruciating pain, was a man marked by absolutely radiant joy, and there is a connection. Father Pio used to go through anguish when he was celebrating Mass. But he was a brilliant, marvelous man, and I'm sure that the bottom line was joy. You read all the great saints, and they suffered like mad. But, my gosh, they came through to some fabulous joy. We don't invite pain, and we don't want pain, but we have to be truthful about it. There's not a simple, superficial answer to the question of pain.

Question: The big question for me is: "Why is my life always failing?"
DEH: Well, in the United States, "failure" is rather a dirty word. But nothing succeeds like failure. You *must fail* as the little one. You die as the little one, and that's ultimate failure. Thank God for failure, which leads you to the only success, which is enjoying Who you really are.

Face to No-Face

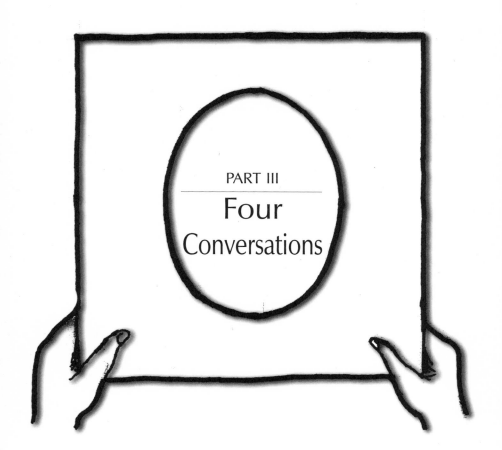

PART III

Four
Conversations

CHAPTER SEVEN
Conversation I:
May 1987

Question: *What is seeing Who you really are?*
DEH: It's so simple, it's difficult to describe. Normally we are looking at other things, but seeing Who you really are is looking at what you're looking out of. It's turning the direction of your attention round precisely 180 degrees and looking at what is nearest of all, what is central to your life—the permanent ingredient in all that you are and do. Namely, what's at a distance of zero inches from you. Usually, I am intent on what is quite a long way off, a few inches or feet or miles off. But Here's a region that I've learned to ignore, under social pressure. I've learned to pretend it doesn't exist, is unimportant, dangerous, and not to be looked at. It is what is right Here—what I'm looking out of.

That's what Seeing is for me.

Question: What are you looking out of? I see Douglas Harding over there. Are you looking out of him?
DEH: Well, Douglas is your problem. I don't see him Here. At the moment, I can see quite a lot of stuff, but I wouldn't recognize it as Douglas Harding. There's a pullover, trousers and shoes, a couple of hands sticking out here, but I wouldn't call all that Douglas Harding. No. What I find Here is Space for that stuff, that body, those clothes and hands, Space for you now, Space for the recording machine and the window and the trees outside. I find Capacity—Emptiness Here which is filled with what is on offer. And what's on offer is very clear and very evident. Primarily at this time, it is you.

Question: So this Capacity is aware?
DEH: Oh yes, certainly it is. It's not just any old capacity, any common-or-garden room for things to happen in. It's very alert to itself at this time as Capacity.

Question: Douglas, how did you come to this?
DEH: I don't know when I came to it. That story about having an experience in the Himalayas—well, I did. I did. But that was not coming to it for the first time. I'm sure I had more than hints of it long before that. So I don't know the answer to that one. How do you come to the thing which you *don't* come to, which you are? That's an odd question. The answer is that I don't know how I came across Myself. It's so built in, so central, I can't say.

Question: In every respect, looking out is different, in fact totally opposite from looking in?
DEH: Yes, that's right. But there is another thing that I must add

here, which is that I can't find any way of separating them. I can distinguish them totally, but when they are distinguished totally, they come together totally. If the view in is anything like the view out, then they never come together. But if the contrast is total, then one is capacity for the other, and the unity is total. I *see* this to be the case. In other words, the Space I have *is* its filling. When I just look out at you, I'm only getting half the story because I'm leaving out the half that lies in This direction. But if I look in This direction, I'm getting the Clarity, and I'm also getting you filling it. So my whole business in life is to look Here because looking Here involves there, whereas looking there doesn't necessarily involve Here. If I do that in my so-called relationships with other people, I have the experience of being them. How am I them? It's a double identity. First of all, I have their appearance, which they apparently don't have for themselves. Secondly, I am Here this Awareness which they are. Here I am you, and you, and you, ad infinitum.

Question: When I look Here to this Space, it's not just "space," is it? It's really finding that I am the aware Source of everything. In other words, I am God where I am. That is so different from imagining I am a person.

DEH: Yes, there are three possibilities. One is that I am what society brings me up to claim to be, namely a human being just like the ones I see around, a solid, normal, perishable, limited object. That's number one. Number two is just space—emptiness for other human beings, sheer emptiness, a vacuum to be filled with things. But there is a third possibility, and it is vastly different from the other two. It is true that no words will compass or describe what I find Here. It is free of characteristics. But paradoxically, this gives it incredible value. There is a saying in the *Upanishads*—it recurs in various scriptures—that we get happiness, satisfaction, peace only from what is open-ended, unlimited, what cannot be comprehended, what is totally beyond our frame of reference. It breaks through from the outside, totally mysterious. From that we get satisfaction; from the limited, never. So the third possibility I'm talking about is the No-thing which really is No-thing, really indescribable. But I am it, and therefore it is the one thing I really know without being able to describe. It is something that baffles me to put a word to. It is what I am. And what am I? I am No-thing, aware of myself as No-thing. But this, being totally mysterious, self-originating, incredible, ungraspable, unknowable, thereby mysteriously becomes what I can put my money on, my infinite Resource. Something so precious, something . . . I just can't find any words to describe it. Can you help me here?

Question: I know the word God doesn't even begin to fit this mystery, yet it has a certain power and gives some indication of Who one is. But it is hard to say anything.
DEH: Well, certain things can be said about it. What comes and goes, what is changeable, that I cannot be, cannot rest in, cannot find my peace in. That is not my Resource. That which can be known is something I can get my intellectual tape measure around. My Resource has to be ineffable, ungraspable, totally convincing, totally precious, but existing for no reason, really. I suppose what gives me the entrée, in a way more than anything else, to this sense of my identity, this identity which is incredibly nothing, and incredibly valuable, is its self-origination. It is the Abyss from which *I Am* proceeds. It's more fundamental, infinitely more fundamental than the sense of *I Am*. It's like the sense *I Am Not*, but it's the fountain—well, it's not the fountain. It's where the fountain comes from. It's the source of the fountain of *I Amness*, which is Myself coming into being. It's below Being.

For no reason. It is the bafflement, the vertigo, the giddiness really of the Godhead investigating its own unknowable origins. The Godhead is totally bowled over by this. And strangely, this ignorance, this not-knowing, is the profoundest kind of knowledge.

Question: Clearly, it's not Douglas seeing this, is it? It is the Source aware of itself with astonishment.
DEH: Here, I can't find anything remaining of that guy, Douglas. He's over there. It is as though one has levels. The bottom level of all is the unspeakable No-thing, the unthinkable Origin which we could call *I Am Not,* from which the *I Am* proceeds. Then proceeding from the *I Am* level, *I am Douglas, I am you, I am the universe.* These are various levels of manifestation. But I feel that my refuge, my resource, my joy, my blessing comes from what is below Existence, below Being, below thought, below feeling, is the "place" from which it all comes. In a way, the Potentiality of everything is more precious than the actuality. Because the Potentiality is so deep, so resourceful, you can rest in it. The actuality is always flying off in beautiful creativity. The point about a fountain is that it is always in motion. But I can't rest in the motion. I have to go back to where it is all coming from.

Question: The No-thingness is so endlessly astonishing. It can never be grasped, held, or understood, and yet it is a resource of such awe.
DEH: And the beautiful and mysterious thing is that just this simple act of turning around 180 degrees puts us in immediate touch with it.

Question: So this Seeing is not a shallow thing. It's a simple thing, but it is looking to the very depths.
DEH: Yes, infinite depths. Looking out into the world, one looks

into a cul-de-sac, into some terminus there. Whether it is the sky
or the trees or you or that desk, the view ends there. But looking
180 degrees the other way, the vista goes on and on forever into
depth on depth of unknowable mystery—above all, the mystery of why and how it contrives itself, how I contrive myself.
It's unknowable. I am quite sure that God's greatest joy is his
own ineffability, and one is one's own evidence for this. A God
that has got himself taped would be so thin, meager, shallow.
This is a most extraordinary joy. How can one express this wonder? How can one do it justice? It baffles one to describe it, doesn't
it? But just turn around, and you're in touch with it at once.

*Question: What would you say about bliss? Do you think it has a place,
a reality?*
DEH: People mean different things by bliss. I can say what meaning I would give to the word. What I've been describing will do.
When I get on to the manifestation of various levels of this creative Source, this Mystery, they don't hold bliss. The bliss is to be
found at the point of origin. There is a *Upanishad* which talks
about *ananda*, joy, or bliss being at the root of everything. It is joy
which creates the world and achieves Being. The very nature of
the Source is joy, and other creatures must live on a diminution
of that joy. So it's as if the world is coming out of joy, but is getting less joyful as it goes on. Well, one has to be in touch with,
has to be the joy from which the world comes. The world, when
taken by itself and apart from that joy, is *dukkha*, suffering. Mysteriously, the suffering is somehow taken care of from its Origin.

Question: Is this joy something that comes and goes?
DEH: No. It is timeless. When I contact it you may say it looks as
though I am contacting it now and not five minutes ago when
we were talking about something else. But when you contact

this region, you don't have a sense of returning to it. You have a sense that no interval exists whatever between the occasions of enjoying it. No interval whatever. The Center of my being is changeless, and where there is no change, there is no time. This then is forever my Reality, not something that comes and goes.

Question: Being this, I am aware that everything is within me, as if my arms are around everything and nothing is excluded.
DEH: Absolutely, and this brings me to the question of our identity, which is the basic question of our lives. There is a great tradition, apparently flying in the face of common sense and modesty and certainly the popular view of things, which says that I am not a man. "My me is God, and I recognize no other," says St. Catherine of Genoa. You have scores of the great mystics, coming from all the great religions, who find their true identity to be none other than the Source of the whole world. One starts off with a provisional identification with this or that, with what one sees in the mirror and so forth. But our undoing, our trouble, is those false identifications. My own way of putting it is very simple and is the language of my childhood: To be saved is to be Him. From every point of view, this works out. Nothing else works out; nothing else is true. Everything but God perishes. Well, am I perishable, or am I made of God, as Dante's Beatrice said she was? It is in some sense just a matter of looking to see.

Question: But in another sense, is it something that grows? Does this sense of identity mature and deepen?
DEH: The vision of it, its direct apprehension, is the same throughout because there is nothing to be grasped. In my own experience, my first view of this is not different from my last. Nor is it different from other views of it, if there are other views of it. In a certain sense, you could look upon others as viewing

this, too. But once you introduce the possibility of levels and degrees Here, we are back in trouble again, very deep trouble. We are even more separate than we were in our humanity. The point is that I can find nothing Here to vary at all. I find no difference, no development. Of course, when it comes to the expression of this in my life and its connection with all the downstream stuff of my life, why then it is capable of ongoing change forever and ever, as far as I can make out.

Question: Do you mean change in terms of your understanding and living of it?
DEH: Yes, but the experience itself is the experience of oneself as infinitely capacious, infinitely clear, infinitely deep, and aware. That is the same all through: timeless, changeless, bottomless, ineffable, indescribable Simplicity. The same in all and for all.

Question: In what sense does this affect what you want, your personal will, your designs? Where does surrender come in?
DEH: Gosh, that is so important, isn't it? It is so important.

Question: Do you have any personal will?
DEH: Well, perhaps surprisingly, I find that Douglas's will or, at any rate, his strong preferences are very much around. I would much prefer to be healthy, and if I'm not healthy, to get better. I prefer a nice day to miserable, cold weather. I prefer that my friends are happy and that things are going well with them. So in that sense I have an enormous array of strong preferences, indeed will. I don't find much change there. At the same time, there is another side to it. Seeing Who I am Here is not only a case of surrendering personal will. It is a case of surrendering the person who has the will. So implicitly and in principle, this in-seeing that we are talking about is already total surrender be-

cause it doesn't leave a speck of anything Here. It doesn't even leave a person to exercise will, let alone will. Here. But it is part of the condition of being Douglas to be out there willing things. It is what makes him Douglas. To pack up that sort of thing would be to pack up altogether. Being human means having a whole host of preferences, and strong preferences too. To pretend that these are weakened is simply saying you are tired of life. It isn't being virtuous. No. Having strong preferences, even to the point of willing things, is perfectly consistent with surrender.

What then is this surrender? It is staying here at the Center, and from the Center surveying all that is going on there, including preferences. It is seeing them from this Position, and taking responsibility for them from this Joy, this strong sense of the Mystery, this strong sense of one's identity Here as the Origin for whom nothing can go wrong, for whom all is well. You see, if I am Who I am advertised to be by the great mystics and the great religions, if I am the One and the only One, the Alone, what can go wrong? And in what sense can my will not be carried out? If I am the Alone, and alone by including all beings, not by excluding any, then my will is done. I can conceive no way in which it can be frustrated. So, in being Who I am Here, I am surrendered to whatever happens because it is basically my will. That is perfectly consistent with noticing that Douglas has got a whole repertoire of stuff that he would like to see happen. It is the living together of these two things which is important. It is not saying that Douglas has to be a milk-and-water saint accepting everything equally, without preferences. Not at all.

Question: We are so deeply conditioned to be somebody, right from the beginning of our lives. How do we get off that person? How do we get to deep surrender, to deeply sensing Who we really are? How do we fulfill our heart's desire in that sense?

DEH: I don't think we can get to it by contrivance, by training ourselves. It is mysterious. I am inclined to take refuge in a word which is seemingly a cop-out—*grace*. It explains nothing. Looking back, why is it that this "seeing business" has been my life? I've been a pretty poor exemplar of the whole thing, but it has been my life. Why? Why should I have elected to go for This rather than to become a successful architect, or whatever? It happened to me in spite of all my resistances to it. I don't know. It is one of those questions I cannot answer. I tried very hard to avoid This and was pushed into it, you could say, by the unsatisfactoriness of the alternatives, by having a very tough time when I tried to do anything else.

Question: Do you think that seeing This helps you as a person, sorts out some of your problems, perhaps relationship problems?
DEH: There is absolutely no question about it. To doubt it amounts to asking if living from the truth is more satisfactory than living from a fiction. Of course it is. You may say that Douglas's life is not so different from other people's. He seems to have a few problems here and there. "Seeing" doesn't seem to sort out his life entirely. No, the answer is to realize that two things are going on. Douglas is peripheral, way out there in the mirror and not Here. But Douglas is a creation of the Center Here, a manifestation of This. Considered on his own, by himself, he is about as crummy as most similar manifestations. But seen and accepted from the Origin, the situation is totally different. The only way we can really see the world is from the Origin of the world, namely the Void, the Clarity Here. That's a very remarkable thing! Now let's see it consciously from its Origin. Seen only at its own level, it is pretty poor stuff, and Douglas is as faulty and as troublesome a character as any other. Yes. But seen from his own Origin, somehow he is OK, and he is in a sense per-

fected. Nothing has gone wrong—which seems a very conceited thing to say. At its own level, everything seems to be flawed, somehow spoiled. Seen from its Origin, not so.

Question: This undercuts the idea that we need to reach some kind of spiritual level before we get enlightened.
DEH: The word *enlightened* is a word I don't care to use very much. But if one must use that word, there are two traditional views here. One is that in order to find out Who you are and become enlightened, you have to polish yourself up, go in for some kind of discipline, become qualified to make this momentous discovery about your identity. This is the end product of a long period of training—months, years, perhaps lifetimes of discipline. A lot of people have believed that and tried to follow that path. But the consensus is that, if ever those people do come to see Who they are, they give a great big laugh and say that all along they were trying to polish a brick till it turned into the mirror that (if only they had realized it) they already were. At last they see that this polishing is all rubbish. They see that all discipline, all achievements, all improvements are totally irrelevant and that from the very beginning they were Who they were and enlightened. Then, of course, there is the other school that recognizes that you *start* with enlightenment, and you go on to deserve it later, practice it later. You start with the easy thing, which is seeing Who you are.

All this spiritual discipline with a view to enlightenment one day is damned difficult. It requires great strength of character. It is in many ways a cramping thing, and it is something you have to pay a very high price for. In total contrast, this inward look, this turning around the arrow of attention and looking within, discovering Here this central Perfection which is one's very source, this is a bit of cake. It is simple and easy, and it is the one thing that I can't make a muck of. Yet it is something we avoid doing.

Question: Why do we avoid it?
DEH: That is a mystery. I suppose that God, having decided that he was going to play hide-and-seek with himself, having decided that he would divide himself apparently into parts in order to experience one day the joy of coming together again, doesn't want the game to be over too quickly. That is one way of putting it. Why individually do we avoid this? We have one fear above all else, and that is the fear of disappearing, of vanishing without trace. We all have a hunch that when we really investigate this thing we have built up Here, we will see that it just vanishes with nothing left. That reads like annihilation, of which we are very reasonably scared stiff.

Question: Going back to discipline, do you think there is any place for it, for practice, or can we just do what we want?
DEH: Meditation and that kind of thing? In a sense, it is indispensable, surely. Here's a paradox. On the one hand, there is nothing to be done; the situation is absolutely right. One is Who one is—nothing can stop or ruin that. Looked at from the Origin, one is perfectly in order. So what is there to be done? Where does the discipline come in? A lot of Zen masters rub that question in: "What are you trying to do? Your trouble is that you think there is some trouble, and if you would see that everything is all right, and relax into that, then all would be achieved." In fact, the thing to be achieved is the idea that there is nothing to be achieved!

On the other hand, having said that, it is also true that sustained seeing Who one is is the most difficult thing in the world. Almost. It is certainly very difficult to maintain this inward look.

Chapter Seven

At first with most people it is something that is hard, even impossible, to keep up. It is intermittent, and one is always being diverted from it. At best, it is frequently interrupted. At worst, it is something we do just a few times in our lives. In a sense, what is wrong with that, since looking into Who one is is looking into the timeless realm? There are indeed no gaps in time between the lookings in, so what's the trouble? Does one need to maintain in time that which is out of time? But we function from the Timeless into the world of time, and that is where the practice is essential. Otherwise, nothing really happens, and seeing Who we are is fruitless, a barren thing, with no consequences for living. In order that the seeing into the Timeless shall bear fruit in time, a very great deal of work has to be done. What is the work? It is not an achievement, not doing something afresh. It is constantly coming back to see that there is no work to do and all is well! It is the turning around of the arrow of one's attention as often as may be. That is the practice.

Question: How do you keep this going?
DEH: You practice this by doing it in all the circumstances of life, increasingly, till you don't need to do it any longer because it is doing itself and going on all the time. You are in touch, sometimes very consciously and vividly, more often perhaps in a subdued way. But you are aware of It; you are not in negligence of what is Here. There is a sense of "Here am I, gone." That's a funny way to put it. Here am I absent, or present as Awareness with no characteristics, as Capacity for the world. The practice is ceasing to overlook the Looker, or the Hearer, the One who is Here.

Question: Do you ever have to make an effort to pay attention to Who you are?
DEH: *Effort* is not the right word, but I can't give a better one.

We have to go on making an effort until we see that effort is quite pointless. It's not an effortful thing at all, is it? It's more like relaxing back into what is forever established. How can we be effortful about something that is already doing very well, thank you very much!

Question: Are there some things or situations which help and remind you to see?
DEH: Very much so. In some situations, this in-seeing is very vivid, and on other occasions, it is present all right but not in a very sharp way. This is perfectly OK. It doesn't have to be brilliantly on show.

Ramana Maharshi pointed out that it is not in its nature to be always sharp and brilliant and very prominent. It is sometimes like a background to life. Well, the occasions which for me are apt to produce the sharp sense of seeing the Space are situations like now. There is your face, and Here is the absence of mine. I have built up over the years a very strong habit of being face to no-face. I needed to do that to get out of the nonsense habit of being face to face, which is never true. It is always a lie, troublesome and productive of all kinds of tensions, fear. So I find it extremely helpful having someone in front of me, a face there, whether I know the person or not.

Question: What other occasions are especially helpful?
DEH: When I experience something strikingly beautiful, like flowers, colors, music, beautiful patterns—very attractive things. But their attractiveness is not about being pulled out and lost in the object. Rightly perceived, they reveal the Subject as much as the object, and the two are absolutely one. Normally, when we say something is very attractive, we mean we are pulled out there. What I'm saying is the exact opposite. With some of this training

we are talking about, these attractive things are also concentrating things.

Question: What about workshops as reminders?
DEH: They are so effective. I can spend an hour, two hours, in a workshop, and my Seeing has been sharp virtually all the time. I don't know whether anyone else is getting a lot out of the workshop, but certainly it is a way of concentrating one's own attention, because you cannot run this kind of workshop without all the while being sharply aware of the absence of someone running that workshop. If Douglas were doing so, it would be quite wrong and fraudulent. So it is a superb opportunity, superb practice, for this attention.

Question: Would you recommend doing the experiments to remind oneself?
DEH: You mean outside of workshops? Well, we are all different. There is no standard pattern. I don't go round pointing my finger Here, and I don't go round putting cards with holes in them on my face. Life is a workshop, and I don't need special contrivances. Life produces just what is needed. But perhaps for those of us for whom this is fairly new and fresh, new habits have to be formed. Using this in-pointing finger, observing the Single Eye—why, that would be very appropriate. And being very consciously face to no-face with friends who share this is really helpful because of the infection that is going on around the room. The reinforcement is tremendous.

Question: What about difficult situations and problems, such as personal relationship problems, work problems, health problems? Do those help or hinder?
DEH: Seeing Who you are has an immense relevance to these

things, though it doesn't dispose or get rid of them. You may even seem to get a special crop of them because you are more aware of what is going on, more sensitive, perhaps taking on responsibilities, like caring for people. You might feel you have a more complex and troublesome life after seeing Who you are than before!

Nevertheless, something very profound is going on. Just as I am looking at your face from no-face, so I am looking at the problem from no-problem. I am Space for the problem. I don't just have the problem; the Space is terribly important. Space is what makes the difference. Until we cotton on to this, there is just the problem. Of course, at the same time that I am Space for the problem, I am also the problem, just as I am your face now. The Space in which your face is revealed to me now is not other than your face. However, the problem is seen from the No-problem.

In very simple, practical terms, it is absolutely OK for the problem to be problematic at this time. It is accepted. When a thing is seen from the Source, it is authorized. It is OK'd. It could be very painful. One could be very ill or dying, for that matter, but when perceived consciously from the Source, the situation is transformed—not by a kind of detailed manipulation but by viewing it from the Place that is free of the problem, from Who one is.

Question: Does this mean that you are not involved in trying to sort out your problem or improve your situation?
DEH: Yes, it does mean not being involved in that. I see the problem as part of the world, and I have no power at all to interfere. I have nothing to do really except look at it as it is given. To change this problem altogether, to remove it, would be to change the whole world because everything hangs together in a web of mutual conditioning. We have got the idea that we can treat the

world by piecemeal action, rooting out this problem and that problem, or at any rate transforming problems. This is illusory. What I can do is to be the Source of the problem, the Source of the whole world, really. This is not to want to change it but to accept it and to see that it is OK. It is a hard thing, isn't it? Suppose something pretty nasty happens. Either one is very ill, or a dear friend is having an awful time, or one's circumstances take a nose dive. What can one do? It depends on what level one is operating from. On a certain level, one must do something. One takes action. But in the last resort, that action is as conditioned as the thing being treated. It would occur anyway, wouldn't it? I mean, these hands will get up to something, these feet will go somewhere, this voice will continue to sound. All that stuff is conditioned. My business is not to fuss about all that. My business is being where it all comes from, consciously.

Question: You are a very active person from this Nothingness. The Nothingness is a creative Nothingness. However, what you are proposing could sound like sitting back and...
DEH: Yes, fatalism—saying I am OK Here, I have no control over what happens, and I am just going to sit at home, idle and uncaring, resigned to what is going on. Seeing Who you are is not like that at all. It is extremely active. After all, Who am I? Who are you? I am action itself. I am this power which is my true nature. This Void Here is the Father and Mother of everything. From This the world is generated. It is really the only energy there is, so I am energetic in this sense. My task is to let all that energy, that power, that creativity flow as it will and recognize and enjoy it. But I feel my pleasure, my job, is not to monitor that, not to try to guide it, change it, get involved in it, but to stay with where it is coming from. Stay with the Abyss, the Unknowable, the Potentiality, not the actuality so much. Then you are

the actuality, too.

The emphasis of identification for me is on the Source. Stay with the Center, and the periphery will be OK. Go for the periphery in negligence of the Center, and you are literally in trouble. Of course, when you look at the Center Point, it expands infinitely in all directions. The Center explodes. But it is the Center you make for.

Question: What are the psychological effects of this Seeing?
DEH: They differ so much, person to person. We all start off with our special handicaps, crosses, and limitations. What is the effect going to be of living this Seeing life on those handicaps? It is quite unpredictable. There are even moods in which one feels as much stuck in the mire and as crummy as ever.

This business of fruits is a hard one. Nevertheless, there are fruits. But if we go for them, if we are too concerned with them, we are in trouble. If you want good fruit, don't fuss about the fruit. Feed the roots of the tree, make sure they are healthy, and the fruits will come. If the ground is parched, you don't water the fruit. You water the ground. The fruits are in time, and the roots are out of time—eternal, dark, hidden. The Abyss—that is the root. You don't know what the fruits will be. Time will tell.

So much agony, nonsense, handicaps, and trouble arise from living the lie, the illusion, that one is a small, limited, temporary, opaque thing Here. The origins of greed, hate, delusion, with all their offspring—fear and so forth—can be traced to it. I get shrunk from being unlimited Space for everything, which I am as an infant, into being this little thing. Now, what is the result of that shrinkage? I am angry because I resent the society that cruelly cut me down to size. I am frightened because if I am a thing, then I am terribly vulnerable to the activity of other things, their hostility and abrasion. Terrified. I am envious of the possessions and achievements of others. The world was mine, but now I am shrunk to this little bit of the world. So I have to be greedy to get it back, to establish again my ownership of it if I can. Of course, it is a hopeless task. All I do is load myself with more burdens in the way of possessions.

So this illusion that I am what I look like is productive of all my troubles. When I start living consciously from the No-thing Here, there is going to be a difference. No longer am I greedy, or very greedy, because if the world is mine, what is the point of collecting little bits and pieces round me to prove it's mine? I don't need to if I see that Here is the Origin of the world and that this Origin is indestructible, eternal. Then where is the place for fear? Where is the place for envy? The fruits grow out of the seeing, though they may be more visible to other people than to myself.

In fact, as Who one really is, I don't think one has fruits. The only fruit I have as Who I really am is this darn great fruit of the whole universe. That is a fruit and a half, isn't it? To talk about little fruits here and there is to confuse Who I am. What am I? Am I little Douglas, bearing a lot of silly old fruits? No, I am the Origin of the whole lot. That's my fruit. That will do me.

Question: You spend your life writing and talking about this, sharing and living it. Do you think the headless way is going to be more accepted in the future?
DEH: Crystal ball now! You know, good things are happening, and counting heads makes sense. But counting No-heads makes no sense. There is only one No-head. Plotinus said a marvelous thing: "Out there the many faces, but here the one Head of all. If we could but turn around by our own motion, or by the happy pull of Athene, we would look in and find here the Self, and God, and the All." As far as numbers go, faces are many, but this

one Head is already unitary, perfect, established. If we look at the time world, we always get a picture of change and development. If we look In, nothing has gone wrong. It is heaven now. There is nothing to be done.

We are not seeing things as they really are when we are worried about the state of affairs now, thinking it's about time people tumbled to this simple thing that we are on to. Why are we not winning more assent from the world? This question is perfectly understandable and natural. But at a more fundamental level, it is absolute nonsense. All that has gone wrong is that we have not seen the world, we have not seen Reality, as it is. Out there the many faces. Here the one Head of all.

Question: Is this inward look an important leap in human consciousness?
DEH: There is, of course, that way of looking at it, which is the evolutionary way. In historical terms and ignoring the timeless Source, we began perhaps five million years ago as very skillful, intelligent, fairly upright animals, anthropoids who didn't see themselves as objects. We were Capacity for the world, just like the Space that a baby is now and that animals are. Then came the great leap forward, taking no doubt many hundreds of thousands of years to develop from a unique and rare accomplishment to a common and then a normal one. A slow, yet for the individual, a sudden leap. We began to see ourselves from out there, as objects among other objects, objectifying ourselves with the help of something like a mirror, the surface of water, probably. Imagine primeval man, like a gifted and adventurous child, pulling faces where he is and seeing the man pulling faces in the water. He finds a correspondence between the nature and timing of the feelings here and the picture in the water. Then he goes on to catch a hold of that face as it were and say, "It looks to

be over there, but it is really Here. Here, I am just like the others. I am what I look like." He has become a human being.

Sorting all that out takes a long, long time, and it is not completed yet because some people—primitive types—have not arrived at that full objectivity. It is an all-important evolutionary leap, producing civilization and the human condition, with all its positive achievements as well as its terribly negative ones. It seems to me that the adventure of the future, which may or may not come off on this planet, is to take the gains of all that adventure into self-objectification and combine them with Self-subjectification, with the neglected original truth which the animal and tiny baby are living from. Here I am the *I Am*, just *I Am*, and there I am Douglas. In other words, I see Who I am. I remain a member of the human club but secretly withdraw my subscription, my subscription being this illusion that I am what I look like. And quite obviously, our friends who see themselves this way are very clearly more human, in a sense, than before.

True humanness is fully achieved when I recognize the difference between my appearance, my functioning out there peripherally as a human being, and the Source Here, which is not human at all. I think that Jesus Christ, who clearly saw that he was one with the Father and was perfectly aware too that he was a carpenter's son, realized this ideal. He was a real human being because he had got both poles of his being sorted out.

Question: How does this fit in with the conviction that one has a mind?
DEH: I am not denying anything for which there is evidence. Psychology and psychiatry haven't got quite the scientific status that physical science has. Nevertheless, there is a lot of evidence for their general findings. The mind is not all imagination. It is a very complex field to study, and a lot is known about it and needs to be known about it.

Face to No-Face

What is my mind? It is interesting that so many of the great
seers and sages of the world have said, "Never mind the mind.
The trouble with your mind is you think you've got one." That is
the kind of thing that Ramana Maharshi said, and at a certain
level, it is absolutely true. But there is a level at which the mind
is perfectly real. Well, *perfectly* is not quite the right word! But
the mind has got a certain reality. Let's look at that.

What do I mean by Douglas's mind? If I really get down to it,
it is not other than my universe. My mind is a very complicated
abstraction from the universe as I find it. In other words, it is the
feelings and thoughts I find attached to the objects of the world.
I am looking at trees now and have feelings about them. I like
them. I have thoughts about them. I name them. I perceive them
as beautiful, perhaps sometimes as threatening—they may fall
down and hurt people. In other words, the world as I find it is
replete with feelings and thoughts, which I can collect or abstract from the scene and put in a "box" Here, as though they
didn't adhere to objects but adhered to me the Subject. I pack
them in a box Here and say I have a mind. I don't find that helpful. I am like the primitive human and, I would say, Ramana and
company. I can't find a mind of my own Here in a box. It is absolutely fictional. I find it far more practical to let my feelings and
thoughts belong where they do belong, which is along with the
object.

In practical terms, to illustrate this, I see that my feelings and
thoughts about you belong to you. They don't characterize me
Here but you there. You are served up to me with color, with
motion, with shape, and with all manner of marks that serve to
identify you. That is the way you come to me. I am not going to
take possession of the affection I have for you and put it in a box
Here. That is a pretence. I can't do it, and in so far as I can do it,
it is sentimentality. It is getting something out of it for myself,

robbing you of it.

So it seems to me that mind, when it is abstracted from the universe, is damaging nonsense. When I take my feelings and thoughts from the world and put them in an imaginary mind box Here, they suffer en route. This separated mind gets me into every kind of trouble, and it is unreal and worrying. There is everything to be said against it. But when it is allowed again to settle on its objects, it is rectified, and it gains very much in being sent back to where it belongs.

Question: You're saying that the source of those thoughts and feelings is free of those thoughts and feelings?
DEH: Yes. What I find Here is free of thoughts and feelings, yet it is absolutely real, and very vividly so. That is very interesting, isn't it? It is totally devoid of thoughts and feelings but totally real. The world as full of thoughts and feelings is a real world, but its Source is free of them, and still more real. The contrast is total.

Question: So this kind of attention, seeing, or meditation is not a matter of wiping out thoughts and feelings from the Center.
DEH: No, it is putting them where they belong. Nor is it a matter of projecting them onto others. The psychologists make great play of the idea of how bad it is to project onto others your problems. For example, say I am a greedy person. Projection means I go around finding other people greedy. I project my greed onto them. We do have this mechanism of finding our own faults in others, instead of taking responsibility for them. But I am not talking about that very choosy, piecemeal projection, which won't do. I am talking about a total projection of the whole, a global projection, which means taking responsibility for all things, not washing your hands of any of them. It is acknowledging that

these qualities of feeling and thought which I project onto the world are mine because the world is mine. It all comes from Here. This is not that "bad" projection, or pushing out one's problems onto the world and not taking responsibility for them. It is quite different.

Question: What about that piecemeal projection and those knots and twists that we find in our characters? What about sorting them out or sorting through them?
DEH: You mean one's own weaknesses?

Question: Yes. Is there a place for therapy, for trying to sort them out, for improving oneself, or for clearing oneself of them in some way?
DEH: I think there is. The question is, how do you do it? I can only do it effectively in one way, and that is to become aware of my weaknesses, very sharply, from the place where there is no weakness—from the Origin. Any idea that by gritting my teeth and somehow determining by willpower to change myself, to improve myself, and to become a saint or a good person, or even a nice person, will not do. One has to be alive to these weaknesses, defects, twists, these screwed-up regions of one's personality, to be perfectly aware of them from Who one is, admitting them to oneself. That will do the trick. One has to look at them from Who one is and, in a way, accept them, as if to say, "Look at old Douglas! What a funny old thing he is!" If I don't fuss about improving him, strangely enough some improvement will come as a by-product of accepting his very amusing, deplorable humanness.

Question: If I am overlooking the Center, I am probably assuming there is someone at the Center. That assumption is bound to upset everything in the end.

DEH: Yes. Why am I trying to reform Douglas? What is the point? The only purpose of value at all is to give people a less difficult time around me. But I am not sure that I can do that. The attempt to improve Douglas is the attempt to foist on him the perfection of Who I am Here at the Center. That is impossible. My motive for polishing up Douglas is very devious indeed. The only safe thing is to be aware of—and to be prepared to be humiliated by—what I find there.

Question: How does seeing that you are not in a body affect your experience of being somebody physically?
DEH: Well, I have a body, but how is it served up? I am not denying anything. I am just trying—succeeding, I hope—to be awake.

How do I experience my body? Well, first of all, I see these legs and hands. My body is around a lot, certainly. Secondly, associated with these legs and hands are a lot of sensations. However, when I look at my body, I see I am not inside it. It is inside me. I am Capacity for it. I am as free Here of my body, Douglas's body, as I am of that recording machine. The important thing is to be aware of the way it actually is presented instead of the way I was told it was presented, which was that I was shut up in it. I am not in it. It is in me. This is the way my body is given, and it is really the healthy and enjoyable way to have it.

Question: So instead of sensing yourself shrunk down into a small thing in the world, you experience yourself as big.
DEH: Absolutely. Unbounded. If I insist on having a body, even looked at from the point of view of function, of what will work, of what is complete, this thing I had identified with under social pressure and was told I was is just not viable. It is not all there. It is just a fragment, totally dependent on air, water, earth, and light,

161

the sun, the universe itself. The only body I have, if I am going to be realistic in functional terms, is the universe none other than the universe. That is my body.

Question: I cannot divide my sensations off from the world. Normally, I would say that my sensations are Here and the world is there, as if my sensations were in a small box. But that is not true. I expand.
DEH: Yes, sensations are global. Particularly if one shuts one's eyes, one can find no boundaries at all. Even with eyes open, there is no way of separating oneself from the world.

Normally, one pretends to live inside an envelope or a sealed plastic bag, moving around along with a lot of other plastic bags in this supermarket of a universe. What's the good of that? A miserable situation. But it's just not like that, is it? The whole thing boils down to the simple proposition—I like coming back to simplicities—that I am NOT what I look like. To say that I am Here what I look like there to you makes no sense. It's absurd. It is a thundering, thumping great lie. What a thing is perceived to be is a function of the range of the observer. When I come all the way up to myself, I lose myself, and I find the universe. The only way I can get Douglas Here in imagination is to be eccentric, to live out there, a meter or so away, gazing in Here at poor old Douglas, central in my life. But it is total nonsense, and we can't do it. That is the human invention, the human fiction. Well, it is possible to be human and disabuse yourself of that idea. Then you become truly human—out there, not Here.

Question: With this Seeing, certain powers become available, don't they?
DEH: Yes. By just attending we find we have powers which are really magical. For instance, I am now moving those trees around. I really am. Many tons are being moved around there. When you say, "Come on, Douglas, all you are doing is swaying on

your chair," I say, "That's your point of view. There is no swaying Here. There is just the trees, and the trees are dancing about
there." When I travel in the car, I am moving the whole country-
side. Billions of tons are on the move. And what is more, I can
stop and start and stop them.

Question: There are many powers, aren't there?
DEH: Yes. I have abolished you and the trees now. Everything is
gone. I now make you reappear. I take that seriously. I think that
God is extremely naive. The great thing is to be as simple as God.
See what is given. This is the marvelous thing. If we would relax
into what is blazingly obvious, we should find all that we need.
It is a kind, kind old world. It hides nothing essential. The more
essential a thing is, the more given it is. We imagine it's the other
way round. What is really important is given free now.

*Question: When I listen Here, I hear the Silence in which all the sounds
are given. I can hear my voice and your voice, and I am aware that both
voices are no distance from me. They are both mine.*
DEH: In a way, one seems to experience control over one voice
and not the other, but if I attend very carefully, it is very hard to
find a difference. In a workshop, for instance, when sounds appear to be coming out of Douglas and then out of someone else,
I don't feel that one of those voices is my voice and the other one
is someone else's. One becomes the Source of all.

All voices are yours, like all faces are yours. A marvelous set-
up. And what is so beautiful—this has really come home to me
in recent years—is that what one needs is simplicity and humility in front of what is given. The more we need a thing, the more
lavishly it is laid on.

Question: When I see that I am the Source, everything appears as mine.

DEH: Well, what is ownership? Things can't own things, can they? Things just knock up against one another. They touch one another. A thing just owns itself, if that. But this No-thing, which is Awareness, owns the world. Truly to own something is to be it—and that is to get out of its way and so become it, to let it fill you. The world is yours that way.

Question: We resist letting go of this little person and everything that this person owns and knows. But when we let go into being No-thing, it is a transformation into a grandeur that is unbelievable. Owning everything, being everything, willing everything through having nothing.

DEH: I am very cagey about talking about detailed and particular results, but seeing This does make all the difference. I can't think of anything that I want other than what I have got. If I could think of anything I'd want, it would be something like a pot of flowers there, but that is just a passing thought. What do I want? It does put paid to acquisitiveness and greed in the most remarkable way. The transformation is profound and total.

After all, what do I want in life? I want something to do. I want adventure. Even just looking at it from an ordinary, common-or-garden point of view, this is a very valid formula or design for living. I have so many discoveries to make. It is so exciting, so surprising to find everything upside down. Can you think of a life that is more fulfilled, more interesting, more acceptable than this? Discovery is such a great thing. People who got a lot of mileage out of their lives and really enjoyed themselves were people like Darwin, Einstein, Columbus. Columbus had a rough time in some ways, but he had some thrills. Think of what we have got here for discovering—everything, because everything is upside down. We have only scratched the surface of these discoveries. When old Douglas packs up—I mean, gosh, get him out of the way!—there will be floods of discoveries coming along. The field is infinite. Does God ever get to the end of his Self-discovery? You mean to say that in a few years, in a lifetime, in the work of a little group of friends, the whole ground has been covered? It goes on and on.

Question: *Douglas, can you sum up in a word what you have been saying?*
DEH: *Attention*. That is the Buddhist watchword, and of course it figures prominently in Aldous Huxley's *Island*. Attention. Another word I like, a magical word, is *awake*. Awake, and not in a coma. It is not about achievement; it is about daring to look at what's on show. How do we wake? How do we stay awake? That is a hard one. But certainly it is about Homecoming. A saying that has helped me recently a lot is: "Only make for the Center, and the rest need not trouble you." The periphery will look after itself if I look after the Center. Another portmanteau word which holds so much is *identity*. There is only one problem, and that is the problem of my identity. All the rest, all life's problems, are subsidiary to that. If I get my identity straight, all comes straight. If I get my identity wrong, all is mucked up. Identity. I know "Who am I?" is a cliché, and I try to avoid it because it has psychological uses. But what is my identity? There are only two possibilities that I know of. Either I am a product of the world, or I am the Source of the world. I am a human called Douglas, or I am the Source of the world. Which am I primarily?

Question: *When I see This, I see that it is the Origin asking itself which it is primarily, not Douglas.*
DEH: That is right. And then, of course, comes the wonder, the surprise, the mystery, the not-knowing. God is the great not-knower. Humans know a lot. They are know-alls. They really

get to know a fantastic amount.

Question: *God is an idiot!*
DEH: God is the universal idiot! God doesn't know. And what doesn't he know? He doesn't know how he does it, how he achieves himself. God is bowled over by the splendor and mystery of her own invention, existence, whatever, and that is the great unknowing. Is it Lao Tse in the *Tao Te Ching* who says, "To know is shallow; not to know is profound." My ordinary knowing is very provisional, an *as if* kind of knowing, sketchy and inaccurate. But that knowing is based on the Unknowing because it is the Unknowing that I am coming from. I come from the Unknown. I am unknown and unknowable. Of course, the knowledge that I am beyond knowing is the real knowledge. To come from that! If I go forward in life thinking that I know a thing or two, thank you very much, and that I am quite a knowledgeable bloke, if I go forward with that kind of smirk of self-satisfaction on my face, oh, how much I am missing! What I am missing!

CHAPTER EIGHT
Conversation II:
October 1995

Question: Some people respond to your message by saying, "That's solipsism," the belief that I am the only one who exists and everyone else is a figment of my experiences. What is the difference between what you are talking about and solipsism?

DEH: There are two kinds of solipsism, a bad kind and a good kind. The bad, or rather unprofitable, kind is little old Douglas saying, "I've only experienced one I, one first person. All the others around me are he's and she's and it's. My I is unique. I've never discovered another I than this I of mine. Therefore, all you lot may be non-I's, cardboard cutouts, dream figures in my life." First, nobody takes this sort of solipsism seriously. It's a game. And secondly, if you could take it seriously, it would be a hell of loneliness and alienation and misery. It's a rotten kind of solipsism.

But there is a good kind of solipsism, which is like the first, and that is to discover that Who you really, really, really, really, really are is the Only One. But it is the Only One by inclusion. The other is the only one by exclusion. The I Here is the I of everyone, the inside story of all beings, whom I embrace in my I-ness because ultimately Consciousness is unique and indivisible. This is the solipsism, if you like, of God. It is the solipsism of Who you really, really, really are, and its other name is love.

Question: Most of your observations have to do with visual experience. Do you see them as metaphors for something broader, or do you see these illustrations you use to make your points as literal?
DEH: They are absolutely not metaphorical, absolutely not gates to something else. This is the direct experience. Jesus said, "The pure in heart shall *see* God." The essential Truth, the central Reality of our nature is directly perceptible. Seeing this is not a means to an end. It is the End itself. When I say that I see, as I see now, that Here I am absent in your favor, that I see Here this Capacity, this Openness for you, which is as wide as the world, awake, empty for filling with you, it is not a picture of something else. It is not a symbol or a metaphor. It is the experience itself.

Question: In reading the mystics, I have noticed that they describe transcendent experiences. But you take ordinary experiences as your starting point.
DEH: This is so important. We need to distinguish between mystical experience and what we are on about. I'm not on about mystical experiences. I'm not on about peak experiences. The books describe—and why not?—all these wonderful peak expe-

riences that people have. But the trouble with a peak experience is that you can't have it when you want it. It's not available at will. It comes by the grace of God. Three times in my life, perhaps, I have had an absolutely devastating mystical experience, like Pascal, who wrote his experience down on a scrap of paper and kept it sewn in his jerkin. Once in his life he had this overwhelming experience.

This is not what I am on about. I am on about the common-or-garden occasions like today when it's all available now, full strength. But it's not excitement. It's not a peak experience. It's more like a valley experience. It's always available because seeing Who I am is not a matter of emotion. It's a matter of direct, simple perception, available when I'm feeling rotten or when I have a tummy ache. It's even more available when I have some problem to be addressed. You say, "Well, can it be really what we need if it is so available?" But in the ordinary things of life is concealed an enormous depth. Seeing Who I am is the sacramentalization of ordinary life. It makes it precious and marvelous. The mystical path isn't a path; it's a great trap. We read the books, and we wonder how we can get an experience like we find there. Or we've had one, and we wonder how the hell we are going to get it back. So we hope and read and read and hope, and we make ourselves miserable because, of course, it doesn't come. To go begging for mystical experiences is bad enough; to flash them is worse. "I've had a better mystical experience than you. He's got a peak experience right up there. I've got to the foothills." We are all at sixes and sevens.

The view that God is revealed in the ordinary, common-or-garden things of life is revolutionary. Not ordinary in the sense of being on the television and in the newspapers and everyone seeing them but ordinary in the sense of being everyday yet truly seen, seen as given, which involves a reversal of everything.

Everything is upside down. I am the exact opposite Here of what I was advertised to be and was told I was.

When we attend to This, when we give up prejudice and dare to look, surprise upon surprise awaits us, concealed in those things which are so wrongly taken for granted. Spirituality suffers from high-flying, woolly, meaningless words and abstractions. Seeing Who you are is bringing it down and having a look. For example, I have a look at how many eyes I am looking out of. Gosh, it's one huge one. It's not a man's eye I am looking out of; it's God's eye. Here it is on show. All we have to do is look in the right place. I don't find hints and suggestions Here of what the secret or truth of my life is. I find the thing itself.

Question: What is this thing itself that is available in perception now that was not available prior to my seeing Who I was?
DEH: Actually, we are always living it. As a child, I was it. Then I forsook it. I imposed upon this Reality Here a picture of Douglas. I looked at myself through others' eyes in my imagination. But what is this Reality Here that I am looking out of? What is it? Well, in our experiments, we don't just stop and give it a name. We notice several characteristics. We go into it. We ask questions. How big is it? It has no boundaries. How empty is it? We see it is immaculate, clean. How full is it? It is totally full. How awake is it? Gosh, it's wide awake. Does it move? No, it never moves. This is an investigation in some detail of the marvels of our true identity, lending tremendous conviction to what we see.

Question: When we do the paper bag, we see the face at the other end of the bag as an object. How do you make the leap from seeing that face as an object to saying that the inside story of that object is the same as my inside story, that it is a Subject as well as an object?
DEH: This sense of others being conscious is so built in to our

lives, we never question it. Why do I do workshops? Why do
any of us relate to each other? We are sure that the other person
is a living, conscious entity. However, in the bag, we seek that
person's Awareness. We look for it in the eyeballs, which is nonsense. Eventually, we look at the near end of the bag, and we see
that the Awareness Here has no personal marks. It belongs as
much to the one at the far end as it does to the One at the near
end. The Consciousness at the near end includes that of the one
at the far end. It spreads out. The face at the far end is soaked in
the stuff because the Consciousness Here is as wide as the world.
It is the world. Consciousness can't be boxed. You can't confine
it.

We all have the idea that the little one is conscious. We think
there are two consciousnesses, the Consciousness of the First
Person and the consciousness of the second person, of the little
one. Well, that's not so. When I look honestly at that little one, I
see he's a picture. Any Consciousness that I attribute to him is on
loan from Here. Awareness inheres in the First Person Here.

The First Person is the timeless Container, indivisible, never
changing, boundless, the *I Am*. Everything it contains is perishing and limited. We must distinguish between the Container and
the content. The Container is like a television screen but without
any boundaries. It is necessary to the program but it doesn't
change with the program. You are the screen.

*Question: I see that the little one is just a picture. It doesn't think or
have desires. And the Big One doesn't want anything. So where do
these desires come from?*
DEH: Perhaps the price of the universe is that God plays a game
of hide and seek, pretending to be separate people in order that
love and adventure and the journey Home can take place. This
idea that we are all split up into separate personalities is indis-

pensable. If we dispense with it, the universe collapses into a unified, perfect deity at the Center. We need the game of pretending in order to have a story. But it is a story, a fiction. It is not true. The ultimate truth is that I am you. However, both are needed. We have to allow the divine descent into particularity and individuality. This descent is not just a human game. It is a divine game in order that love should come into the world. It is a hugely costly and painful game, but who would have it otherwise?

Question: *Where do all the desires come from, then?*
DEH: They are part of the game, aren't they? What helps is to ask not, "Is it true?" but, "At what level is it true?" The truth of one level is the nonsense of another level. Ultimately, there is only one Consciousness. Only God exists, the *I Am*, the One. It's true at that level, but we can't live at that level, nor does God wish to live at that level. The other levels occur and are very, very precious and essential to the story. At these levels, we are pseudo-separate individuals, thereby giving love an opportunity to flourish. You have been given the little one to look after as a unique incarnation of Reality. This is not a way of writing off that one but of giving that one a divine preciousness.

Question: *The story you are telling of the One and the many sounds like* Vedanta. *On the other hand, Buddhism says there is no such thing as the Container of the experiences or no such thing as Awareness separate from the experiences. There is a big distinction between the two views.*
DEH: There is indeed, but we must distinguish between Theravada and Mahayana Buddhism. In Theravada Buddhism, the Buddha says that metaphysical questions should be left on one side and that we should look at the ordinary things of life

and see how we can make our lives more tolerable, avoiding suffering and desires. This has its value. But in Mahayana, the famous *Heart Sutra* begins, "Hail to the Prajnaparamita, the perfection of wisdom, the lovely, the holy." Then it goes on to say, "Here, oh Sariputra, no eyes, no nose, no mouth . . . Here, form is void. But the void also is form. Therefore, we cease to tremble." So Buddhism itself not only produced something very much like God, but it even goes ecstatic about it. What I find attractive in Buddhism is rather the Mahayana. But even in Theravada Buddhism, in the Pali Canon, in what purports to be the older and more basic tradition, you find sayings about Nirvana being marvelous, wonderful, accessible in this very life to the wisest.

In any case, while I have great respect for the great religions of the world and their exponents, what they say is hearsay. It's in books. I was told it. I am going to do what the Buddha said and be a light unto myself, taking myself to no outside refuge. He says that in the Pali canon; it's supposed to be his last words. I do that. I test the scriptures by my experience. Then I say the Buddha got it right. It may sound conceited, but I don't think it is. We see what the truth is in our own experience and then go to see if the scriptures got it right. If they got it right, we enjoy that. We can then get a lot of refreshment and companionship from them.

Question: It's relatively easy to disappear in favor of someone you love and to feel loving toward that person. But you have no guarantees the person you face will love you. They might be torturing you and go on torturing you till you are dead.

DEH: The way Christianity and other religions have of looking at it is that I accept what happens to me from Who I am, from God. If I take everything that happens to me from the One, then even the unpleasant stuff I say yes to. If I take it from man, it's going to be impossibly hard. If from God, terribly, but not impossibly hard.

Question: *If someone is torturing me, I can't not disappear in favor of that person.*
DEH: It isn't easy. There's no pretending that it's automatic. That's why we need to get in much practice while things are comparatively comfortable.

Question: *Do you believe in an afterlife?*
DEH: My business in life is to get used to being Who I really, really am instead of just being little old Douglas, for whom one life is plenty. I've got to put in my practice now. Plato said that philosophy is the practice of death. That sounds miserable, but in fact it isn't. I've got to practice being Who I am now, in my heart giving up being Douglas.

Question: *God cannot be pure Awareness without having something to be aware of, surely?*
DEH: That's right. God, to be God, needs an object. This is what the Christian doctrine of the Trinity is about. God's love and admiration and wonder is not poured out on Himself, which would be rather like Mohammed Ali beating his breast and saying, "I'm the greatest!" It would be no more admirable in God than in Mohammed Ali. It's love poured out on the Son, as the Son's is on God. This is a true picture of the nature of love and reality. The Subject needs an object. The Subject is not a Subject until it has an object. This pseudo-split is indispensable.

Question: *So at the same time as God creates himself out of nothing, he is creating something to be aware of.*
DEH: Exactly. It's marvelous, isn't it? There's no love without an

object. Loving yourself is not love. There must be a certain otherness. Eckhart says, "God is a not-God." God gives himself up for the object. We are made in the image of that One who disappears in favor of the object. It's so true, and it's so incredibly beautiful. It seems to be contradicted by everything in the world. Nevertheless, we are built in that image. The First Person disappears in favor of the second and third person.

Question: I am concerned because in American culture there is more focus on the little one than ever before. That could lead to the end of things as we know them on the planet. That's scary.

DEH: The ultimate truth is that we all live from the Truth. We are all open This way. Most of us just pretend otherwise. One *cannot* close oneself up. Everyone is busted wide open. It is very important to notice that we are all doing it right. This prevents you from feeling superior. If other people seem to say, "I'm doing it right, but I don't wish to know I'm doing it right," it's their bad luck and their responsibility. But they are living from This. Everyone must live from This. Otherwise, they would be running into buses and falling over the furniture.

It is the human condition, not just the condition of Western culture, to be unaware of oneself and to imagine oneself a separate little thing, closed up. It has been like this all over the world for the last few hundred thousand years. Now we've come to the end of that game; it's time to blow the whistle. This vision of our Openness used to be the province of some rare, disciplined people, probably celibate, living very ascetic lives. Now we have the tools and the need and the urgency for This to become normal—not universal, but normal—so that a person is not reckoned mature until he or she sees into his or her Space.

Question: My first question is: Since Who I really, really am is Void, how can something which is nothing have a will? My second question is: Given that there is a way for this Void to have a will, and this Void is also love in the sense that it is disappearing in favor of the world, how can it be that it is the will of the Void to have a war that is killing tens of thousands of people in Bosnia? The suffering in the world is endemic. How can it come out of this pure love?

DEH: When we look at reality or being in its true, pure nature, the One who just *Is* has no will. Angelus Silesius says that God has no will. God is Consciousness alone. What we call the will of God is downstream of God because it is changing. It occurs in time. One wills this; one wills that. It varies, so it's not central. We distinguish between what is at the Source and what is downstream of the Source. The will is downstream of the Source, though it's pretty near the Source. So you are quite right. For himself, God has no will. He is Awareness.

However, God gets up to the business of willing and producing the universe, and both the will and the universe are downstream. Then you say, "What a crummy old world! Does God will events in Yugoslavia?" This is a mystery. I don't pretend to give a complete answer. But my feeling is that the price of a universe is the plus and the minus, the negative and positive. God would have just adored and loved to have created love without hate, beauty without ugliness, truth without lies, but could no more do that than he could create left without right and up without down. God was not free to create a world which was all positive and not half negative. So the world that God willed and imagined was the world of these built-in contradictions of plus and minus.

You ask what kind of a God it is that creates this suffering world and is sitting pretty up there washing his hands of all this horror. Well, that would be a horrible and terrible set-up. But my reading of it is that God comes down all the way to the sink and basement of the world, to the Bethlehem stable, and to the place of crucifixion, and gives his life for the world. And you say, "What evidence have you of that?" I have the evidence that I am built in that image, to give my life for the world—not because I am nice, not because I'm a good old Douglas. One is built to this blueprint. The world is structured around self-giving love, or self-giving disappearance in favor of the object.

The price of this world is very high, for both God and man. It was a limitation of God's omnipotence that he couldn't create a universe that was all good. He would have loved to have done it. Anyway, could you have adventure without danger? Courage without the possibility of disaster?

Question: I understand that you cannot have good without bad, but why does it have to get so bad that six million Jews were killed in concentration camps?
DEH: There is a mystery in suffering. There is a contradiction. It is an amazing thing that from suffering comes something which is unattainable by any other means. I don't understand it, and I'm sure God doesn't understand it. But suffering is not what it seems to be. Somebody left in my house years ago a book called *In God's Underground* by a Lutheran pastor who lived in Rumania. For his beliefs, he was imprisoned in a hell as bad as any Nazi concentration camp. Most people died, and it was absolutely ghastly. He didn't think he was ever coming out, but he *was* let out after fourteen years in this horrible place. And the sequel is unbelievable. People asked him what it was like coming out of that, and he said it was like coming down from a glorious mountaintop into the very unglorious world. He said that the secret of survival and joy in that place was saying yes, yes, yes. He took everything from God and nothing from man. He paid a price, my God, but he transcended somehow the suf-

fering, and came through into peace and joy.

And then there's another piece of evidence here of a different kind. For me, the greatest play of Shakespeare is *King Lear*, a terrible, terrible tragedy. But, you know, it gets to one's heart in a way nothing else could. I'm not saying I'm happy about suffering. Suffering is awful, and I'm very bad at bearing it. But we have to realize that there is a mystery and a contradiction here.

But these are big questions, and at the end of the day I have to say I don't know. Let me ask questions that can be answered, like: How many faces are there in the bag? Are the telegraph poles moving or am I moving? Or have I anything Here to keep you out with at this moment? These are answerable questions. We spend our lives, if we are philosophical types, asking ourselves questions which are unanswerable and neglecting the questions which can be answered. That is what the Buddha objected to. Me, too.

CHAPTER NINE
Conversation III:
November 1995

Question: Are the selfish impulses meant to disappear when we learn to live from Who we are?

DEH: This is a fascinating and crucial topic. When someone says something that I find myself denying or being irritated by, two responses are available to me. One is just a cross, "Douglasy," self-regarding one, and the other is the cool, First-Person one coming from Who I really am. This duality presents itself not all the time but a lot of the time.

I have little Douglas there with his limited goals and interests and motivations, not only around but active. To deny this is dangerous because it is suppressing the facts and pretending that I am not what I am. It's covering the thing up instead of bringing it out into the daylight and looking at it and coping with it. We have a real association with the little one. Part of it is a proper caring for that one, which is absolutely legitimate. The other part, which is the more dubious, challenging, if not sinister part, is the residue—more than a residue—of pettiness, irritation, boredom. I wouldn't say anger, I wouldn't say fear, certainly not fear, but residues of those naughtier aspects of Douglas. They have value, which is to bring me back Here. They are signals that I am overlooking or tending to overlook what is Here. To be aware of them, really aware of them, is to draw their sting, largely.

Question: You say that these negative feelings are indications you are overlooking Who you are. In other words, if they arise, you are not really seeing Who you are?
DEH: Well, it's a strange thing. It seems they *can* arise while I'm seeing Who I am, even vividly seeing Who I am. Something occurs which is giving me a bit of a problem. I'm irritated with something, but it doesn't necessarily indicate that I'm not vividly seeing Who I am. At other times these negative feelings might indicate that I'm not attending with sufficient care to Who I really am. It doesn't necessarily mean I'm overlooking Who I am. There's a very extraordinary saying by a noted Zen master (which doesn't make it true, of course), which runs like this: If you can see into your Buddha Nature without dismissing greed, hate, and delusion—the three stains—you can turn these devils into angels protecting the *dharma*. So these devils—greed, hate, and delusion—seen from, examined from, Who you really, really are, in some subtle way change their character from devilish to angelic. It's very strong, isn't it? Very reassuring.

Question: How do you interpret that?
DEH: It's an exaggerated way of saying what I've been trying to

say, that negative feelings are not abnormal but natural, and whether you are honest about it or not, nobody, however holy, practiced, or disciplined, is free from them. While that little guy in the mirror is still there in the mirror, that is what he is like; he's doing his stuff. Even Jesus was irritable and rude. He got angry, he cursed fig trees, he upset the moneychangers' tables, and he called the holy men of his time a generation of vipers and whited sepulchres. He was an extremely vulnerable, somewhat bad-tempered chap. I don't know whether this proves that he saw himself as such, but when somebody called him "Good master," he is alleged to have said, "Don't call me good. Only God is good."

Question: Many traditions assert that you can tell whether people are seeing Who they are by their moral quality.
DEH: This is absolutely true, and I wouldn't deny it. "By their fruits shall ye know them." All the same, spotty and unripe fruits are perfectly consistent with sainthood. Dom John Chapman says: "Every saint is sure he's a pig." What makes sainthood is not perfection. What makes a saint is humility and love. Thérèse of Lisieux, for example, confesses to being very, very irritated with one particular sister. The joke is that this sister came to her eventually and said, "Thérèse, why is it you love me better than the others?" Now, the modern dictum is that you have to voice your irritation and not bottle it up. I'm on the side of Thérèse here because she really did love that sister in the deepest sense, though she was very irritated by her. Then again she says somewhere that there is a great wall between her and God, a great wall that she had great difficulty getting through. It's a fiction that in this life the little guy can be radically reformed. In fact, one seems to get worse, not because one *is* getting worse, but because one is more sensitive to the tricks and subterfuges and games of that little one, much more aware of them than one was

before. It seems one is getting worse, but it is not so.

Question: Do you make a distinction between seeing Who you are and living from it?
DEH: No. To see Who you are and do it day in, day out, would issue in living it. If it's an intermittent thing, or something you put on for mixed motives, like running workshops and getting applause and attention, then you aren't living in the light of that vision.

Question: If you see Who you are persistently, that will lead gradually to deeper levels of surrender?
DEH: I think so, yes. Surrender is not an absolute thing. It grows or should grow. It is never incapable of further deepening. It is something you come to gradually.

Question: Can you give me an example from your own life of what surrender has meant to you?
DEH: Well, yes. On this trip, the responses of the folks at the workshops have been very disappointing. Am I feeling miserable or resenting this? I can honestly say I am not. I have surrendered to the possibility that the whole trip might be disappointing—and not only the whole trip but the rest of my work so that, far from succeeding in getting the message around, I may find the reverse happening, and my work from now on may go downhill, outwardly. I'm convinced that in the long, long, long run, in so far as it's true, it's going to work and win. I've no anxiety about that. But I have surrendered to the possibility of its not coming to anything outwardly in my lifetime. After all— I know this is perhaps a naughty analogy—how long was it before the crowd which was shouting "Hosanna in the Highest!" and spreading branches in the triumphal entry into Jerusalem

was shouting "Crucify him!"? His twelve friends all forsook him at the last minute. That took some surrendering to.

There's an element in Douglas which likes having books read and publishers wanting more stuff and the meetings full of enthusiastic people. There's an element of Douglas wanting that, and it can't be got rid of. I don't think it should be got rid of. When one has a room only quarter full, that takes some surrendering to. But once one says yes to an unwelcome thing, one sees that it has enormous value. One could be a failure in worldly terms, and the joy and the comfort, the security and peace that come of this vision, regardless of anything that happens out there, is enhanced, not daunted at all, by that outward failure. It's the only example I can think of. But surrender always has to be renewed. It isn't automatic. If it's easy, it isn't surrender.

Question: Some years back, you went through a period of particular difficulty.
DEH: I think that was different.

Question: But in On Having No Head, *you talk about the Barrier in connection with surrender, as the barrier of will.*
DEH: Yes.

Question: Did you learn something from that which has stayed with you and made surrender easier?
DEH: It's mysterious. I don't really know. Some people don't come up violently against the Barrier. For others, it's an intermittent collision which goes on for a long time. Though fairly brief, it was, in my case, a near-psychotic episode. Very crazy. I suppose it had value. I really don't know very much about this. But I'll tell you one thing which is significant, perhaps. The chapter in Evelyn Underhill's *Mysticism,* which I read again and again

and again with joy, or at least with tremendous appreciation, is not the last one, which is "The Unitive Life" but "The Dark Night of the Soul." Strangely enough, that seems a good place. All the spiritual attainments, all the certainties, have dropped away, and you are left resourceless and in despair, empty, lost, unable to feel anything that is positive. For me, it was a feeling that I was so awful, so without any merit, so deplorable. I was a write-off in the eyes of God, man, my friends, everybody. It didn't last very long, but it was very nasty. It was needful that one should go through that dark night because then one can understand what happens in other cases. It gives one a certain insight and compassion into what does happen in people's lives. We need to know that.

Also, there is in the Garden of Gethsemane and the Crucifixion this unavoidable experience of the basic suffering of the world.

Question: Are you saying that it is not a personal thing?
DEH: Yes. In some sense it is feeling the cost, to God, if you wish, of the world. The cost is very, very, very high. It seems impossibly high. It was a very bad time.

Question: Do you think about it?
DEH: No, not now.

Question: Life is a humbling experience.
DEH: It certainly is. But then it is also an extremely exalting experience. You know, it's despair of that little one which brings me back to joy, to the Big One, to amazement. My current feeling is one of enormous gratitude and wonder at the multitudinous proofs of one's identity on every side, piled up, piled up, showing me Who I am. I think particularly of this wide, wide

Face mounted on this little body, the width of this single Eye, and the stillness, the brilliance of it. It puts everything else into perspective. I am thankful Douglas is so faulty, so constituted as to bring me back to Who I really am.

Question: You said that you have pettiness and irritation but that you don't have fear?
DEH: Well, I would have fear of large, hairy, black, swift spiders, and standing on the edge of a sheer cliff. That kind of physical fear I have plenty of. But, no, fear is not something that happens to me much. The other things, like pettiness, irritation, I have. But one doesn't take them so seriously, does one? It's as though one stands back from them. There he goes again! It gives you an element of freedom and detachment if you are aware of those goings on, fully aware of them. They go with the human condition.

And there's this consideration: who are the people you love, who are the people you admire among your friends, your Seeing friends particularly? Are they the ones who are perfect? Could you imagine what it would be like to have a friend who was absolutely perfect, who never had any weaknesses? It would be awful. He or she would be a monster.

Question: When I am feeling resentful, does that mean I am identifying with the little one?
DEH: We have to go by our own experience. My experience is that when somebody says something that makes me cross, my reaction is pretty standard. I'm seeing Who I am very clearly at that time, but it doesn't immediately make me all accepting of that person, and the crossness doesn't magically, suddenly vanish. Not at all.

Question: The Devil's advocate would say that if you were really seeing who you were, you wouldn't have got cross to begin with.
DEH: Well, that is the view I'm contesting.

Chapter Ten
Conversation IV:
May 1999

Question: *The Dalai Lama emphasizes compassion, reaching out to others, empathizing with their suffering. However, you emphasize truth, not compassion. What about compassion?*

DEH: Sometimes I begin a workshop with a drawing of a crossroads. At the center is Who we really are, our Goal, seeing into our True Nature. The road coming in from the top is the seeing way, symbolized by an eye. The second road in to the center is the way of devotion, symbolized by a heart. The third road is the way of service; its symbol is a hand. Those are the three traditional ways. I add a fourth, the way of beauty, which is very important. Mozart tells me something about God that only music can tell me.

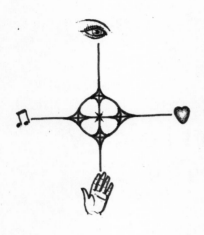

Each of us has by temperament a favorite way, a way that is right for us. Obviously the way for Douglas is the seeing way. But the conclusion I have come to is that one way without the others is very liable to go wrong; it needs the other ways. Fortunately, there is a turning circle around the center, which enables us to get from any one of these approaches to the others. When one way is not working particularly well because of bad weather or road repairs, we're diverted round to go in to the center via another way, thank God. So what was for me originally a linear seeing path is, by the grace of God and the exigencies of travel, turned into a convergence on the center from all four sides.

Question: Practically, how do you move from being on the seeing path only to being also on the path of compassion?
DEH: It just happens. I don't have to say, "Now I'm going to be compassionate or I'm going to be of service." If I am loyal to my way Home and sufficiently in earnest about it, somehow I will be directed to approaching the center also from the way of love, the way of service, and the way of beauty.

Question: So whereas the Dalai Lama has specific techniques for developing compassion, you're describing a chain of events that sounds like grace. You are not offering techniques.
DEH: That's right.
 The story of Ramakrishna, a great Indian sage of the last cen-

tury, illustrates well how the four ways can become integrated into a life. At about the age of nine, he was walking through the paddy fields of Bengal and saw against the dark sky white birds flying. He went into total ecstasy and passed out. The way of beauty had brought him to God. All his life he was subject to raptures brought on by the beauty of the world. That was his initial way. It is a lovely initial way. The next you hear of him, he was a priest in charge of a temple devoted to the Goddess Kali, the Black Goddess, who destroys with one hand and creates with the other. He was totally devoted to the Goddess Kali, who for him represented the Source of the universe. He put her to bed at night and got her up in the morning. He was a very simple man, a marvelous man, in love with God. So he now had two ways home to the Center. What happened next was that a naked sadhu, a wandering holy man called Tota Puri, arrived at the temple. Tota Puri went up to Ramakrishna, stuck a sliver of broken glass in his forehead, and said, "Meditate on that." This time Ramakrishna passed out for I don't know how long. When he came to, the Goddess Kali had found someone else to look after her. Ramakrishna was dedicated to this formless meditation from then on, though I don't think he gave up in the slightest degree the way of devotion or the way of beauty. But he added this, the seeing way. Finally, what about service? Well, the Ramakrishna Mission, which he founded, is devoted to the service of humanity. So he boxed the compass. He came in from all directions.

I do feel that any one of these ways without the others is very liable to run into trouble. The devotional way can run into trouble when you get held up on the guru, or on Jesus as a human being. The guru stands in the way of your arriving at the Center. The guru says, "If you can't see Who you are, surrender to me, and then later you'll be able to surrender to God." But many, many people just get stuck on the guru, don't they? The way of works, of service, is even more tricky. Its practitioners tell me what I need. Look at what they did in Spain under Torquemada: "These heretics and Jews need the flames of Earth to warn them against the flames of Hell." So what did the Inquisitors do? They barbecued thirty thousand out of service to them! Think of what awful things can happen without the modifying of ways other than one's own way! We need the correction of all the other ways. The way of beauty is perhaps the least dangerous of them all.

Question: Do you have any tips, given the shortcomings of the way of Seeing.
DEH: I don't know. It's very useful to have lots of curiosity and quite a lot of problems. The question is, when I think I've done enough of one way, do I have a go at one of the others? I think not. I suggest that if you are really faithful to your way, something like the grace of God or traffic conditions is going to send you round the other ways.

Question: Can you say more about the way of beauty?
DEH: Your favorite pieces of music, your favorite paintings, or the flowers at this time of the year, the colors—don't they speak to you, don't they tell you something indispensable about their Origin? Don't they have the perfume of their Origin? A universe that can come up with a great Mozart aria is that kind of universe. You judge a bush not by the roots or the thorns or the leaves but by the flower. Isn't that aria one of the loveliest flowers of the bush of the universe? Judge the universe by the flower of the universe, that incredibly beautiful aria.

Question: Art always points back to that which is seeing the art.
DEH: Yes. We need all ways to be complete and rounded. Allow

all ways to happen.

Question: Surely it's not true Seeing if it doesn't awaken compassion and service and a love of beauty.
DEH: The Seeing is always available, even when I'm miserable, cross, tired, or bored. I don't find the love equally available. To say that I've got to love someone doesn't work for me. But the Seeing, if persisted in, is the avenue to the loving, and the Seeing is under my control. The loving, apart from the Seeing, is far less under my control. So it's marvelous to have something I can do, something I can always do, and that is just to have a look.

Question: For the Buddha, however, the compassion for all sentient beings came first. His awakening came much later under the Bodhi tree.
DEH: We are all different. Some of us are very good in the compassion department. Others are not so good, and better in the Seeing department. Temperamental differences do come in here. We must allow for that and be compassionate about that!

Question: When we speak about compassion, we may assume that people know what it means and have the same idea about compassion. I find, generally speaking, that this is not the case. One person's compassion can be another person's malodorous act.
DEH: Or sheer sentimentality!

Question: Equating behaviour with insight is not useful. To ask if certain actions are compassionate is really tricky ground. We need to see beyond acts to consequences. It's very difficult.
DEH: I can't cope with all these complications. Simplistically, perhaps, I think that I have one thing to do. If I have two, three, four, five things to do, I'm in trouble because I have to alternate

between them. I have to say, "Now I have to go to number three because number three has been neglected." I have to go back and forth. No. I say I have only one thing to do: to come Home, be Home, and see what happens from Home. That is perhaps what is meant by "Seek ye first the Kingdom, and all these things shall be added." It's marvelous to have one thing to do, isn't it? A problem arises: just come Home and see what you get up to, what you say, what your hands do, where your feet go. And if you are really going Home and acting from Home, what you do will be appropriate for that occasion.

Question: A problem arises when we start gauging how close we are to an ideal state: "Today I had a good day. I got really close. I almost reached it." That process is one of the bewilderments that many of us find ourselves in. Buddhism, beautiful as it is, often is interpreted as a process-oriented philosophy where people sit and then afterwards think, "I really had it there. But then I came back to my family, back to the office, and it went." The simplicity of having no head is not about having or not having an "experience." It's simply about seeing the way we see anyway, acknowledging what we already do without labeling it as a special activity.

DEH: Absolutely true. And a good example of it is the Dzogchen scripture, which has become rather fashionable here in the West. It talks about our ordinary consciousness being the naked Awareness that underlies all, the Clearness of our Nature—such a beautiful, simple thing. But somebody was telling me that when you go to some of the people for whom this is *the* scripture, they say, "Right, you've read the scripture. Now, what's the next step? Twenty-thousand prostrations!" So much for our ordinary consciousness! Well, I'm all for prostrations, but I'm not for their getting in the way of the simple vision. It's too simple, too clear, too obvious, too available for most of us. Shakespeare wrote about man being "most ignorant of what he's most assured, his glassy essence." We don't achieve this. Let's just relax into it.

Question: I have friends who have seen Who they are and have then gone back to the twenty-thousand prostrations, saying that seeing Who they are is too austere, too lonely. They want a community.

DEH: I suppose what really makes a difference is whether you are doing your twenty-thousand prostrations because you think they are necessary to get you Home or whether you are doing them as a rather enjoyable fruit. Are you doing them as a means to a future end, or are you enjoying what is now? It seems to me that once you've clearly seen Who you are, to indulge in the pretense that you have not arrived is something which is not only unnecessary but rather sad. You get Home and you say, "I'm not really home." I suppose it's partly because you expect a Homecoming to be a mystical experience; you expect it to be a peak experience. Of course, it's a valley experience.

Question: The first time I met you, I found the vision too simple. I was into meditation at the time, and I thought I had to bust my ass doing that. I didn't appreciate how simple the vision has to be. Then over the years, it dawned on me more and more that it's just very simple. The simplicity finally overcame all the complex thoughts—just the basic looking back and seeing No-thing. I finally accepted how simple it really is.

DEH: It's encouraging to hear your story. I feel ineffectual very often, not knowing whether people whom I have met just once have gone on to value the simple experience of Seeing. Of course, my business is to make people not need Douglas. I help you get rid of me in your life. Once you are fixed up with the Simple Source, who needs peripheral Douglases?

Question: In many practices, one is travelling toward the goal; one learns by degrees. With this practice, there isn't anywhere to go because one is already there. One recognizes that this is the way one is always Seeing.

DEH: That's right. We are all living from the Center. It's not an achievement. We awaken to what we are already perfectly seized of. To find that I am the exact opposite in all important respects of what I have been advertised to be and what society and language and Big Brother tell me I am, to find that I'm not just different from what they told me I was Here but that I'm the exact contrary—it's so interesting. Such a funny situation, so dramatic and astonishing! I'm told I'm little old Douglas, but I am boundless. I'm told I'm opaque, but I'm transparent. I'm told I am looking out of two peepholes in a meatball, but my Eye is single and wider than the world. I'm told that I move around in the world, whereas, in fact, Here's the still Center of the moving world. In the plane and the train and the car, it's the country that's doing all the moving. This topsy-turveydom is so interesting, isn't it? The trouble with some meditation—of course I'm being a bit naughty here—is that it's so *boring*. Whereas the facts are so thrilling. What is meditation, anyway, but essentially attention, looking to see what's going on, shifting from concept to percept. Looking to see. Not looking to look but looking to see. I have found a very nice quotation from Ramana Maharshi: "I see only what you see, but I notice what I see." I have also found another authority who said almost word for word the same thing: "I only see what you see, but I have trained myself, Doctor Watson, to notice what I see." Sherlock Holmes. I put in a plea for the charm, the interest of this continuous discovery. I've been in this line of business for sixty years, but new things keep coming up. It's an interesting life, a lively life.

Chapter Ten

Question: Do you feel that you always see Who you are?

DEH: That's a good question. I'm going to give you a rather devious answer. When I'm talking about the Vision, as now, thinking about it, writing about it, I couldn't be clearer about what's Here. But when I filled in my tax returns earlier this year, was I consciously noticing taxes-there-to-no-taxes-Here? I wasn't! I was doing the taxes there. You could say, "Oh Douglas, you were overlooking Who you were!" Well, not so! When one is deeply convinced of This, and living from It, occasions are always arising when one needs to concentrate very particularly on something there, like tax returns. It's as if the vision were on hold. It's in the background. Ramana Maharshi used to say it's like the bass accompaniment in music, not the treble melody. You would notice if the bass accompaniment stopped. If I said, "Oh my God, I've got to keep looking at You all the time, even when I'm doing the tax returns," that would be bondage. God is free to rid himself of God a bit. Who we really are isn't under written contract to be one hundred percent and every moment totally engaged in Samadhi. A certain amount of play comes in. Freedom.

Question: It's refreshing to hear that.

DEH: I remember many years ago walking in the woods near my home in a state of great desperation because I kept on forgetting Who I was from time to time. I frequently found myself slipping back into third-personhood. The shades of the prison house would keep descending on me. How could I keep the Vision alive? It was a desperate state. In the end, I decided that I *couldn't* keep the Vision going at full strength. I just gave up. I said, "I can't do it." Then when I gave up, it was all right. I didn't have to keep the Seeing at high tension all the time. It's there in the background whatever happens. It really is, even when I am filling in my tax returns.

Face to No-Face

Question: Seeing Who I am is so effortless that when I catch myself trying to do it more, thinking that I must do it more, that actually takes me away from the effortlessness of just noticing. And if I stop for a minute and see the thoughts that are going on about needing to try or losing it, then that's just something else that appears in the Space.

DEH: In workshops, I'm constantly finding people who say, "Well, I had the Vision in a previous workshop, but then I lost it." This is absurd. Once you've seen it, you know where to look, how to look, what to look for. You've no excuse for neglecting or overlooking it. In fact, they're not saying they've lost it. They're saying they've lost the feeling of it, they've lost the euphoria, they've lost the joy of it or the initial, emotional thrust of it. Of course, that will go. Yesterday afternoon, there was a lady who was obviously in ecstasy about it. I said to her, "It will go." The Vision won't go, but the ecstasy will.

Question: I remember the initial period when the Seeing was so clear. There was a sense of euphoria, of bliss, which went on for quite a while. It was easy to associate that state with Seeing.

DEH: Exactly.

Question: Partly, the euphoria was relief about not being the doer anymore.

DEH: When the penny dropped for me sixty years ago, it was not euphoria at all. It was the certainty that my life was going to be about This. It was very, very cool. It was not ecstatic. It was actual factual. This was good because if it had been a huge mystical experience, it might have been a trap. Pascal, who wrote down his wonderful mystical experience on a scrap of parchment and sewed it into his jacket, never had the experience again. It became archeology.

Chapter Ten

Question: You said before that Seeing wasn't a peak experience but a valley experience...
DEH: Well, it can be a peak experience, by accident or grace. But in its essential nature, which can always be got back to, it's a valley experience. I am nothing Here, absolutely cleared out. When I look in a mirror, at least I exist there. Douglas may be decrepit, ancient, with very little shelf-life left, but at least he's around! There's *something* there! But This—all's gone! You can't get more *valley* than that, can you? It really is the bottom line. Of course, this zero point is also the point of expansion to infinity. Nevertheless, this is essentially a valley experience, isn't it?

Question: In her book, Mysticism, *Evelyn Underhill describes the traditional mystical path as beginning with the high of Illumination but eventually descending very low to the Dark Night of the Soul. In your* On Having No Head, *you also map out a path which includes the low point of the Barrier, where you come to a place which has nothing to offer except the experience of No-thingness. In my own life, there have been times when the experience has been euphoric, full of meaning, but there have been other times when there has been none of that. The Seeing has still been available, but it's the simplicity at that point which I have to value, not any of the feelings or rewards, which have gone. Is this place of emotional lowness built into the path?*
DEH: What all of us experience at root is exactly the same, the same, the same, whatever our paths, whatever our backgrounds. But the routes to it are very different and numerous. You don't hear much about the Dark Night of the Soul in the Eastern religions, but you do in the West. There are these traditions. There are these temperamental differences. We must allow for very great differences in our humanness. But of course, what a joy it is that at Center we are absolutely free of all those differences. Here I am you.

The practical value of this remains. I don't care what I do, I make a muck of it if I think I'm doing it as Douglas, as that little guy in the mirror. What I do consciously from the Center Here— I don't say it's well done, but it's certainly better done. So from a practical point of view, we have this secret formula for doing what we can do, for being what we can be.

Question: *When I do the paper bag, I realize that I really don't know much about myself.*
DEH: That is absolutely valid. I've lived with Douglas for ninety years, and I just don't know anything about him. To know him would be to know all the universe. Look at what conditions him. What am I without my genes and chromosomes, my blood chemistry, all that stuff down to quarks? And what am I without all the bigger stuff—Mankind, Life, the Earth, the Solar System? To know Douglas, one would have to know the whole shooting match. To imagine that I know what I am as a human being is absolute, total rubbish.

I don't know how I do anything, either. When I lift my arm, millions and millions of little chaps are doing it for me. I've no idea how I do it. They get on with the job. When I'm speaking, they're getting ready for the end of the sentence before I'm sure what it's going to be.

To talk about Douglas psychologically is an equally dubious enterprise. But when I look Here, this is perfect Vision. I know Myself absolutely. If I may use the term *God* without being chucked out, I know God. The *only* thing I really know is God. By *God* I mean our "glassy essence," Buddha Nature, Atman-Brahman. I know Who I am, utterly. This is the only knowledge. I can *see* Who I am. I can't even see Douglas because he's so complicated. When I look at my face in the mirror, all those hairs and pores and lines and spots are changing all the time. Anyway, that's just the front view, and only a little bit of the front view. What about all the other views? I can't see him. I glimpse him. I think I know him. I don't. He's a total mystery. But Who I am shines with incredible brilliance because its very nature is to do so. We think that we know our humanness and that we don't know our divinity. It's the other way round.

When we join the human club, we agree to downgrade and abolish the distinction between the First Person and the third person. We third-person ourselves as members of the club: I am what I look like. The First Person, for all intents and purposes, is not different from the third. But of course, the fact is that the First Person is the exact opposite of the third person. If you look in the mirror, you see the exact opposite of what you are like. This is a very sharp way of putting it. And who is the First Person? There is only One. It is First Person Singular, Present Tense. Kierkegaard said that we are all born as First Person but very soon we are blunted into third-personhood.

The Big Guy, Little Guy Experiment goes into this. The hole in the card represents what the infant is to herself. That's stage one of our developmental process. Stage two, which happens to the growing child, is a mixture, an alternation between the Big One and the Little One. The child has joined the human club but hasn't paid the full subscription. She agrees that, for others, she is the little one in the mirror, but for herself, when she is happy, she is the Big One. A marvelous time in our lives, isn't it? The third stage is when we cover up the hole in the card. I lose my Space, and I become my face. I get shrunk overnight from being worldwide into being this little, perishing box. Of course, in the fourth stage we see that this never really happened. We are primarily the Space for ourselves and a face for others.

Question: *Would you agree that one of the reasons we close ourselves*

off in the third stage is to encapsulate our worries into a small, manage-able box and keep out all the troubles and miseries of the world?
DEH: Exactly.

Question: But when we see Who we are, we are busted wide open to all that suffering.
DEH: As the little guy, I have tunnel vision. I say, "I've got enough troubles of my own. I'm only interested in the great world out-side insofar as it serves the purposes of this little guy. I've got enough suffering of my own; I don't want to know about yours." Then something happens—good luck, the grace of God in my case, whatever it might be—and our angle of vision widens and we take on the suffering of the world. The strange thing is that you get beyond suffering by taking it on and going through to the underlying peace which passes understanding. Some people seem to suggest that when you see Who you are, there is no more suffering. On the contrary. In a way, it's the exact opposite of that. You take it all on. You take on the pain of creation, not only human suffering but the whole tragic history of the world and the suffering of other creatures—not because you are a saint or a good person. You have no option. That's the way you are made, and that's the way through. You could say that the rem-edy for suffering is homeopathic.

Question: How can we bring this into our lives? I'm working with men who have battered their wives. Here's a roomful of men with enormous pain, men who have been tortured from childhood on with self-hate and abandonment from both inside and out, and then they turn around and do what's been done to them, automatically. I can't say to these men, "Look, you haven't taken on the suffering of the world, and that's the problem, so open yourself to the suffering of the world. They're not going to understand that because they know their personal lives are filled with suffering. All they want to do is get rid of it. What can I do with them?

DEH: The first thing you should do—and you know this better than I do—is to be absolutely Clear and see Who you are when you are with them. I don't really think I can tell you or anybody can tell you or you can tell yourself what will occur when you are in front of those people. But when you are in front of those people and seeing Who you are, you will know what to do at that moment with those particular people. This is a spontaneous way of life. It's not setting up rules about what we should do on certain occasions. Let the occasion arise, see Who you are, and find out what you do.

Question: I suppose if I allow myself to experience the degree of pain in the room and respond to that pain in the way I feel…

DEH: You can't have a genuine preview of what is appropriate and what you will do on that special occasion. On that special occasion, you will be given what to say and do, and it will be right. It might even shock you and surprise you. I often find myself thinking, "Gosh, did I say that?" This is not a life according to any kind of rule book, however good a rule book it might be.

The fact that these men are socially regarded as very bad men—I suppose they really are—does not necessarily mean it is harder to show them the truth than it is to show the ordinary man in the street. They might be *easier* to show the truth to! You don't know, do you? My experience is that some of the people who "ought" to see this—intelligent and serious people who should be concerned with Who they are—are in fact the most difficult people to share it with! And people who are quite unadmirable and miserable and unintelligent are easily cracked open. If you took a butterfly net and went out into the streets of

Oakland and collected ten people and brought them in here and said that you would like to show them This, you would show more of those ten people than if you collected ten meditators from a meditation hall and tried to show them. People who have a very strong philosophical, spiritual position and value it and try to live it, quite understandably are not going to open themselves to something as simple as This. I've found that sharing This with the ordinary, casual customer (someone I'm sitting next to on the plane who asks me what I'm up to, for example) is a piece of cake.

In my experience, sharing it is the finest way to keep it going. Pushing it at people is always counterproductive. One will know when to share, how to share. It's incredible joy to share it. No other joy is quite equal to that. Incredible joy.

But this is a minority movement. What are the chances of it taking off? Well, I don't actually see why it shouldn't take off. After all, the big turnaround was perhaps a million years ago when some woman, probably, looking in water, had the notion that she was like the people around her. She discovered that she had a face Here. She turned round and looked at herself through other people's eyes, and that was the beginning of the human game. Well, what you and I are doing is simply to complete that operation, moving in—from being self-conscious as a thing at one meter to becoming Self-conscious as No-thing and everything at zero meters. No doubt the initial turnaround took a long time to become popular or general, but it did. Why shouldn't its completion happen, also, in time? If the Vision were one day to become common, or normal, Utopia would *not* result. We all see Who we are here, but we're not *quite* perfect humans, are we? But I don't see why Seeing Who one is shouldn't become normal in the sense that one's development would be measured against that norm. To see Who you are would be the normal completion of your maturity.

Question: It's easy for people to see Who they are. That's not the problem. The problem is whether people value This enough to live from it.
DEH: That's right. Being able to see it might become very common, but living from it is sure to be far less common.

Question: I don't think we are at an evolutionary place where we can expect people to live from this vision. Ken Wilber says that the most revolutionary thing we can expect at this stage is for people to develop healthy egos. Jesus and Buddha are so far ahead of the ordinary person. They are pointers to where we as a species may be going, but it's not possible for ordinary people to live this way.
DEH: But I think we are a pretty ordinary bunch of people here, aren't we? Are we very special? I don't think so. I think we are rather common or garden.

Question: Don't you have to have a healthy sense of self and have certain material comforts and some of your basic needs met in order to be interested in some of these things? I don't think we realize that we are privileged. Very many people don't even have loving parents, or even one loving parent.
DEH: But this doesn't necessarily prevent them from seeing Who they are. On the contrary, it might be the motivating thrust to the Vision. Some of the friends whom I have shared this with have had incredibly difficult lives. Some of them have been alcoholics or have had grave personality defects of one kind or another.

Question: When you say it might take off, I think of how we are barely out of tribal consciousness. So few people are even interested in this stuff.

DEH: Is something so obvious as this going to be ignored by intelligent, fairly normal people for the next several millennia? If it became general knowledge that one's own Center is the Source of the world and that it's accessible, if this became common currency of thinking and feeling among the cutting edge of the race, it would be a tremendous advantage. And I don't see that that's impossible. Why should it be impossible?

But there's a more basic consideration, which encourages me. What I find so ultimately thrilling is the arrival of Consciousness for no reason. The Self-origination of the One is not improbable or amazing but "impossible"! As Heidegger says, there should be nothing at all. But Consciousness, Who you really, really are, for no reason and with no help, is emerging from chaos and dark night and nothingness now in this room as you. The One who can set up and get off its own launching pad, raise itself by its own nonexistent bootstraps out of nothingness—tell me what's impossible for that One. That One is YOU! Getting people to see Who they are is a tiny detail for that One, isn't it? Surely.

Question: How did we get so disoriented? Why is the obvious Vision that would be such an immediate solution to our problems so challenging?
DEH: Well, when we overcome this craziness, what joy! To lose your head, you have to have it.

Question: Yes, maybe that's it. We have to get our heads screwed on right first before we realize they don't need to be there.
Question: But it's an impossible task to get them screwed on right!
DEH: In the card experiment—the Big Guy and the Little Guy—there has been a recent development. You know how you put the card on and see that you are through to the Immensity. Then you look around and see that everyone else is stuck in his or her

card. If all the humans on the face of the Earth were in the room doing this card experiment, you'd still be the only one who was through! That's for taking seriously. Let's go by the evidence. On present evidence, I am the unique One in the whole world. Otherwise, I am lost. As Douglas, I am here today, gone tomorrow, like grass leveled by the scythe, so brief and unimportant. But I see I am the One!

But there's a danger lurking here. That Douglas should think he's the One! Ah, but we have a correction coming along. With my left hand, I hold the card onto my face and see that I am through to the Immensity and Uniqueness. But in my right hand, I hold a big mirror out there, and I see that Douglas is stuck in the card like all the others, like a little marmot looking out of its hole in Switzerland, squeaking at you. There he is. So I am through to Who I am *as Who I am, not as Douglas*. That's very important. It's very reassuring, too. I am sure I'm through to Who I am. Why? Partly because old Douglas is not involved in the process. If he were, I should doubt the whole thing. He's held at arm's length, playing Belgian Nuns along with the others.

What I'm apt to forget is that when I see Who I am, it's not Douglas who is doing it; it's the One who is doing it. And this One is doing it as and for and on behalf of all others; therefore, the effect must spill over onto all sentient beings. I can only see Who I am as the One who includes all those people who "can't" or "don't" see Who they are. It's affecting them profoundly. Here's a reason for tremendous optimism.

Question: Transcendental Meditation has the idea that when two or three people are chanting their mantra together, the vibrations spread through the neighborhood.

DEH: That is unambitious. It's only concerned with communities on Earth!

Question: You've mentioned the No-thing as being timeless. The timeless aspect of it is something I return to frequently. There's an enormous sense of peace Here. All the change is there, wonderful, fascinating, interesting, but Here there's none. When I get worried or excited, I do so about the change there. When I return Here, I experience great relief.

DEH: In terms of that wonderful hymn, "Change and decay in all around I see, O Thou who changest not, abide with me." We despair of "the common man," but what is the hymn he chooses to sing at the soccer Cup Final at Wembley but exactly that wonderful hymn, "Abide With Me." He isn't as shallow as he seems. "O Thou who changest not, abide with me." Gosh, yes. We all need the timeful and the timeless, don't we? As the Hindu scripture says, "Those who only look out are in darkness. But those who only look in are in greater darkness." It's their combination, the union of the timeless and the timeful, that is our healing.

Question: Thank you so much, Douglas. It's been a real treat to hang out and talk together.

DEH: Communication between people who see Who they are is a different deal from communication between people who are playing games, waiting for an opportunity to be heard, saying things in order to establish the fact that they are there. It's something very important and wonderful. Thank you.

About the Author
and Editor

DOUGLAS HARDING was born in Suffolk, England in 1909 into an evangelical Christian sect called the Exclusive Plymouth Brethren. Growing up, he was restricted from ordinary contact with the world. This included not being allowed to socialize with children who were not in the Brethren, read novels and newspapers (he read the Bible, of course), or go to the cinema. Increasingly he questioned the theology and the way of life of the sect until at twenty-one he apostatized, setting out to discover for himself the truth behind all religions. In order to do this, he began an extensive survey of philosophy, religion, physical science, and psychology.

During this period, Harding also practiced architecture in London and then served in the Indian army as a major during World War II. It was at this time that he made the original, empirical discovery that is at the heart of his philosophical work. Consequently, he suspended his architectural practice and spent eight years—twelve hours a day, seven days a week—working out the implications of his discovery. This culminated in the publication of *The Hierarchy of Heaven and Earth* in 1952. The Saturday Evening Post then commissioned Harding—alongside Bertrand Russel, Aldous Huxley, and Paul Tillich—to write an article for its *Adventures of the Mind* series. Harding then wrote *On Having No Head* (published in 1961 and later expanded and republished with a foreword by Professor Huston Smith), in which he relates his insight to Zen Buddhism. Subsequently, Harding returned to architecture, working for several years in

India and then in Suffolk, England.

In 1969, Harding retired from architecture to devote his energy to communicating his message in a variety of ways. He taught comparative religion and philosophy for Cambridge University, using as text his own *Religions of the World*; wrote *The Science of the First Person* (1974), in which he showed how " pre-scientific wisdom dovetails into the contemporary science-dominated scene"; produced the interactive *Toolkit for Testing the Incredible Hypothesis*—a collection of experiments that enable readers to experience his original, empirical insight and which formed the heart of workshops that he was increasingly conducting; and designed a three-dimensional model of the universe called *The Universe Explorer*, based on the diagrams with which *The Hierarchy of Heaven and Earth* is illustrated. In addition, he contributed numerous articles to scientific and religious journals such as *Transactional Analysis Journal, Architectural Review*, and the Buddhist *Middle Way*.

Since then, while continuing to conduct workshops around the world and write articles for journals, he has written several books: *The Little Book of Life and Death* (1988), which develops the implications of his philosophy in relation to death (foreword by Ram Dass), *Head Off Stress* (1990), which does the same for the topic of stress management, *The Trial of the Man Who Said He Was God* (1992), an extended exercise, in fiction, in the proof of the basic tenets of his work, *The Spectre in the Lake: A Modern Pilgrim's Progress* (1996), and *Look for Yourself* (1998), an anthology of his articles. In 1999, an unabbreviated facsimile of his opus major, *The Hierarchy of Heaven and Earth*, was published. All these books, articles, models, and workshop experiments stem from the original insight he had in India.

DAVID LANG is a professor of English and Communications at Golden Gate University in San Francisco, California. A student and close friend of Douglas Harding for more than thirty years, he writes regularly about and conducts workshops on the "Headless Way," sharing with others the immediacy and simplicity of seeing Who you really are.

To find out more about the "Headless Way" and the work of Douglas Harding, contact:

The Shollond Trust
87B Cazenove Road
London, N16 6BB
ENGLAND

E-mail: headexchange@gn.apc.org
Website: wwww.Headless.org

INNERDIRECTIONS PUBLISHING is the imprint of the Inner Directions Foundation—a nonprofit, educational organization dedicated to exploring authentic pathways to awakening to one's essential nature, in the spirit of Self-inquiry.

Our activities include publication of the highly acclaimed *Inner Directions Journal* and a distinctive selection of book, video, and audio titles that reflect clear and direct approaches to realizing *That* which is eternal and infinite within us.

These publications reflect the nondualistic "ground" from which religions and spiritual traditions arise—the Infinite Consciousness that lies at the Heart of all.

To request information or a free catalog of publications call, write, or e-mail:

INNER DIRECTIONS
P.O. Box 130070
Carlsbad, CA 92013

Tel: (760) 599-4075
Fax: (760) 599-4076
Orders: (800) 545-9118

E-mail: mail@InnerDirections.org
Website: www.InnerDirections.org